Kokutai No Hongi

Cardinal Principles of the National
Entity of Japan

TRANSLATED BY JOHN OWEN GAUNTLETT
AND EDITED WITH AN INTRODUCTION BY
ROBERT KING HALL

HARVARD UNIVERSITY PRESS
CAMBRIDGE · MASSACHUSETTS
1949

LONDON · GEOFFREY CUMBERLEGE · OXFORD UNIVERSITY PRESS

KOKUTAI NO HONGI

PREFATORY NOTE

On December 15, 1945, General Douglas MacArthur, Supreme Commander for the Allied Powers in Tokyo, forwarded to the Imperial Japanese Government his historic Shinto Directive, AG 000.3 (15 Dec 45) CIE. Its formal title was "Abolition of Governmental Sponsorship, Support, Perpetuation, Control, and Dissemination of State Shinto." It was more than an attempt to separate Church and State. It was a direct attack on the very essence of the official national philosophy. Paragraph *1h* of this directive specifically forbade the governmental circulation of the *Kokutai no Hongi* (Cardinal Principles of the National Entity of Japan).

What is this book, singled out from among the thousands of Japanese volumes which might be considered subversive as the particular object of attack by the Occupational Authorities? Why has it, of all the militaristic, ultranationalistic, and Shintoistic writings authorized by the Japanese Government, been banned by name?

The *Kokutai no Hongi* is a puzzling and contradictory document. It is obvious, blatant, official propaganda. Yet it is a tortuous argument based on the mystical, poetic mythology of the Japanese Imperial Family. It was published in immense quantities and distributed most widely throughout the Empire, yet it is composed in a prose so difficult that few of the people to whom it was directed were able to read it understandingly. It was itself an interpretation of the educational philosophy embodied in the Imperial Rescript on Education, yet its ambiguities and preponderance of classical references made necessary an extended list of additional commentaries. Its avowed purpose was to combat the social unrest and intellectual conflicts which sprang from the "individualism" of the people and to substitute a devotion to the "national entity" which it identified with unswerving loyalty to the Imperial Family. It was used as a manual or guidebook for teachers of courses in ethics (*shūshin*). It served as the norm by which was measured compliance with the ideological demands of the Bureau of Thought Control. It was an official statement of internal policy, and by implication a prediction of international policy. The *Kokutai no Hongi* today is one of the significant historical documents of this era. It was a milestone in Japan's march to military conquest and collapse to total defeat.

CONTENTS

APPENDICES

EDITOR'S INTRODUCTION

Editor's Introduction

The *Kokutai no Hongi* first came to the editor's attention during a Brazilian raid on a clandestine Japanese school in the town of Marília in the Alta Paulista region of the State of São Paulo, in August of 1940. The school was located in a secret room formed in the concrete foundation of a public building which the Brazilian Government had confiscated from the Japanese colonists. It was taught by a former Japanese naval officer and enrolled the teen-age and younger children of the Japanese workers in the coffee plantations. The copy was lying, together with other treasured articles, in the *kamidana,* or God Shelf, above the head of the instructor's bed in a little alcove at the side of the classroom. Found under such dramatic circumstances, the volume would have excited much more interest than it did had it not been overshadowed by the lurid militarism and ultranationalism contained in the textbooks confiscated on the same raid. No textbooks known to have been used in government schools in Japan itself during the War remotely approached the degree of vicious militarism and blind patriotism exhibited in the teaching materials found in the Japanese underground schools of Brazil.

In the spring of 1945 the editor, while serving as Chief of the Education Section, Internal Affairs Branch, Civil Affairs Staging Area, was charged with preparing plans for the control of Japanese civil education during the expected occupation. The importance of the *Kokutai no Hongi* as a political and educational policy document was then fully recognized and a rough translation was begun under his direction. The personal copy of Dr. D. C. Holtom of San Gabriel, California, was secured and used for this study. Dr. Holtom had brought the volume from Japan immediately prior to the attack on Pearl Harbor and had independently translated some portions in connection with his studies of Shinto. A photostatic copy of another edition in the possession of the Office of Strategic Services was used in translating the final chapters of Book II of the *Kokutai no Hongi*. Japanese capitulation came before the rough translation was completed, and the partial document was flown to Japan.

Early in November 1945, while the editor was serving as Chief of the Education Sub-Section of the Civil Information and Education Section, GHQ, SCAP, in Tokyo, work was begun again on the *Kokutai no Hongi*. Mr. John Owen Gauntlett, a British subject of Anglo-Japanese ancestry with degrees from the University of London and The American School in Japan, was then on leave of absence from his position as Lecturer on English Linguistics at Waseda University (Tokyo) and Keiō University (Tokyo) and was employed as an official translator-interpreter in Occupation Headquarters. He was asked to undertake a new and definitive translation of the volume. Unfortunately, before this translation was completed, the editor was assigned other duties and Mr. Gauntlett was moved to other translation projects. It was agreed, however, that an entirely new translation should be undertaken as a personal and unofficial effort. This was completed by Mr. Gauntlett in Tokyo and final editing was done in the United States, in part at the School for Asiatic Studies (New York), during the editor's tenure as a Guggenheim Fellow engaged in research on Japanese education. This is the text which constitutes the present volume.

The original writing of the *Kokutai no Hongi* suffered almost as many vicissitudes as did the English translation. The original draft was written sometime before 1937 by Dr. Hisamatsu Sen-ichi, professor at Tokyo Imperial University[1] and outstanding scholar in Japanese classics. Dr. Hisamatsu survived the War and the purge of the first year of the Occupation. He gave evidence of his desire to coöperate with the Occupation Authorities by conducting a brilliant investigation of the degree of phonetic writing existing in the earliest extant manuscripts of classical Japanese literature, in

---

[1] Now known as Tokyo University. The word "Imperial" has been dropped from the titles of all universities of Japan as a result of the Occupation.

connection with an official study of the possible simplification of the Japanese writing system. Dr. Hisamatsu's original manuscript of the *Kokutai no Hongi* is unavailable; hence its contents can only be surmised. It is certain, however, that it differed markedly from the final official text, since the manuscript was twice rewritten; once by an official Compilation Committee of technical experts, and once by Itō Enkichi, chief of the Bureau of Thought Control of the Ministry of Education. It is a matter of record that Dr. Hisamatsu was highly displeased with the changes.

The official Compilation Committee which rewrote the original manuscript included the following members:

Yoshida Kumaji	Member of the Research Section, National Spirit Cultural Research Institute, (NSCRI).
Kihira Masami	Member of the NSCRI.
Watsuji Tetsurō	Professor, Tokyo Imperial University.
Inoue Takamaro	Member of the NSCRI.
Sakuda Sōichi	Professor, Kyoto Imperial University.
Kuroita Katsumi	Professor Emeritus, Tokyo Imperial University.
Ohtsuka Takematsu	Official compiler of materials for the History of the Reformation.
Hisamatsu Sen-ichi	Professor, Tokyo Imperial University.
Yamada Yoshio	Professor, Tohoku Imperial University.
Iijima Tadao	Professor, The Peers' School.
Fujikake Shizuya	Professor, Tokyo Imperial University.
Miyaji Naokazu	Official in charge of historical researches.
Kōno Shōzō	President, Kokugakuin University.
Ui Hakuju	Professor, Tokyo Imperial University.

Three of these men have died (Yoshida, Kihira, and Kuroita), and two have been purged, i.e., forbidden to hold public or educational office (Inoue and Yamada).

A second board of ten specialists was established to do research and to assist in the compilation of the book. The board included the following members:

Yamamoto Katsuichi	Member of the NSCRI.
Ohgushi Toyo-o	Member of the NSCRI.
Shida Nobuyoshi	Assistant, NSCRI.
Ogawa Gishō	Chief, Investigation Section, Thought Bureau.
Kondō Toshiharu	School Inspector.
Yokoyama Shumpei	School Inspector.
Shimizu Gishō	School Inspector.
Fujioka Tsuguhei	Supervisor of Libraries.
Sano Yasutarō	Supervisor of Libraries.
Fujimoto Manji	Supervisor of Libraries.

Five of these have been purged (Ohgushi, Shida, Ogawa, Kondō, and Shimizu).

The basic Purge Directive, SCAP AG 091.1 (4 Jan 46)GS, "Removal and Exclusion of Undesirable Personnel from Public Office," directs the removal from public office and exclusion from governmental service of all persons who have been "active exponents of militaristic nationalism and aggression," and in Appendix *A*, "Removal and Exclusion Categories," Paragraph *G*, defines such undesirable personnel as including, among others, any person "who by speech, writing or action has shown himself to be an active exponent of militant nationalism and aggression." It is perhaps significant that those members of the two compilation boards who have been purged were not excluded from public office because of their connection with the preparation of the *Kokutai no Hongi*, but because of their inclusion in other categories of unacceptable personnel. There is no record that the Occupation Authorities evidenced interest in the authors of this document during the first year and a half of the Occupation despite the fact that the *Kokutai no Hongi* was considered sufficiently perversive to warrant its suppression by name in a directive of the Supreme Commander for the Allied Powers.

A possible explanation of the official indifference evidenced by the Occupation Authorities may be found in the character of the final editing. First, in accordance with traditional practices of Japanese official scholarship, a very considerable amount of rewriting was done by the anonymous functionaries in the Ministry of Education. Ostensibly these men were research assistants of the public figures who are credited with the work, and as such were considered to have made little more contribution than had the copyists and clerks. Actually, however, these minor employees were frequently as able and well educated as the avowed authors, and did in fact contribute a considerable proportion of the creative effort. No evidence is now available as to the extent of authorship which must be credited to them in the final draft of the *Kokutai no Hongi*.

Finally, the chief editor, Itō Enkichi, chief of the Bureau of Thought Control and later vice-minister of Education, made such drastic changes in the manuscript, even to the extent of rewriting large sections after the document was in galley proof, that the official published form of the *Kokutai no Hongi* is generally conceded to be the product of his personal labors. Mr. Itō, if he were today available, would unquestionably be purged on any of several counts, including his leadership of the infamous bureau officially credited with instigating more than sixty thousand arrests for "improper thoughts" in the seventeen years prior to the surrender. Death, however, has spared Mr. Itō this indignity.

It was inevitable that the *Kokutai no Hongi* should be compared with Adolf Hitler's *Mein Kampf*, the basic blueprint of German totalitarianism and aggression. Certain obvious discrepancies are evident. The *Kokutai no Hongi* was an official statement of national policy, having no evident personal authorship. *Mein Kampf* was the private philosophy of an individual, assuming the prestige of a national policy when political events elevated that individual to a position of unchallenged and ruthless dictatorship. The *Kokutai no*

Hongi avowedly limited itself to establishing the norms for the social and political thinking of the Japanese, while *Mein Kampf* was a dream of political power that recognized no geographical limits. The most fundamental difference, however, lies in the fact that the *Kokutai no Hongi* is an expression of Japanese thought which finds no counterpart in Occidental philosophy.

Hitler's emotional retreat into the mythology of ancient German culture was never a vital part of his political thinking. His plan of conquest was cynically realistic. His propaganda machine devised, tested, and applied aberrant ideas with the same unemotional precision that his scientists exhibited in creating physical weapons. Few, if any, of his more important followers paid more than perfunctory lip service to this mythology. The *Kokutai no Hongi* is a literary expression of ideas equally aberrant but sincerely held by a very great majority of the Japanese. It is futile to argue that "intelligent" Japanese could not possibly believe such propaganda. This document and similar ones produced after the rise of the militarists to power in the middle 1930's may be more emotional, more vehement than earlier scholarly works, but it is based on an identical belief in the divine origin of Japan, its people, and its ruling family. Without being drawn into an unprofitable philosophic discussion of what constitutes "belief," it is enough to say that, measured by any standard of acceptance which is recognized in Occidental thought, a very high percentage of the political and intellectual leaders of Japan gave evidence of believing sincerely the basic tenets of Japanese political philosophy, the divine infallibility and the eternal succession of the Imperial House. This was not based on a superficial propaganda nor on reason, but on religious faith. It has been charged, and it possibly is true, that the great Japanese leaders in the Meiji Restoration manipulated the revival of State Shinto (Kokka Shintō or Jinja Shintō) because they recognized the political desirability of encouraging a religious fervor in the people's loyalty to the restored Emperor. Whatever the motives of these nineteenth-century advisors of the Emperor Meiji, their work was well done. If in fact these early expressions of belief were not entirely sincere, many of the Meiji advisors and a majority of their successors came to believe their own propaganda.

One of the greatest difficulties for the Occidental appraising Japanese thought is that of reconciling Japanese logical analysis with an apparent acceptance of basic premises which are unsupportable in the same logical system. In part this is due to the vagueness of the Japanese written language, which tends to become a series of isolated ideas represented by the individual Chinese characters, each having a relatively determinable central meaning but each surrounded by increasingly vague connotation. These ideas are strung together only in part by the syntactic structure of the sentence, but to a pronounced degree depend upon the synthesizing action of the reader's psychological context. In part the apparent inconsistency of Japanese thought is probably traceable to the mysticism of Buddhist and Shinto religious heritages. Where the average Occidental carefully segregates the mysteries and inconsistencies of his religious faith from the realities of his political and professional life, the Japanese lives constantly under the influence of these mysteries and inconsistencies. His mere existence as Japanese inexorably binds him to an infinite chain of interlocking events all stemming from the divine origin of the Imperial Ancestors. The only reason for his existence is that he may play the role of an unimportant part in the all-important whole of Japanese national existence. Loyalty to the Emperor and to the traditions of the Imperial Line becomes not a duty but the object of life itself.

When the practical decisions of everyday life are based on so tenuous and mystical a concept as that of the divine origin of the Japanese Imperial Line, some rather ludicrous and occasionally tragic results are inevitable. Thus, for example, there was at least one Christian pastor who preached that "all men are sinners," was tried, convicted, and given a suspended sentence for lese majesty on the grounds that the Emperor was a man, though of divine ancestry, and hence by extension a sinner. Until the rise of war hysteria this was probably an extreme case. The Second Coming of Christ was a doctrinal crime because it was in direct opposition to the concept that the Japanese Emperors must reign supreme for eternity. There were numerous authenticated instances of public officials, especially in education, who stumbled in their reading of an Imperial Rescript and were severely punished for disrespect to the Emperor and the Imperial Ancestors. Members of the Nihon Romazi Kai (Japan Romanization Society) were imprisoned without trial, and in at least one case died of mistreatment, because they had advocated rewriting historic utterances and Rescripts of the Emperors in phonetic *romaji,* or Latin script. No building could be so erected that a common citizen might "look down on" the Imperial Palace.

The *Kokutai no Hongi* was published on March 30, 1937, although the first edition, following Japanese custom, bears the printing date of March 25, 1937. The first printing of approximately 300,000 copies[2] was distributed to the teaching staffs of both public and private schools from the university level to the lower cycle of elementary schools. A notification was sent by the Vice-Minister of Education to all Prefectural Governors, University Presidents, and Principals of *kōtō gakkō* (higher schools, preparatory to the university) and *semmon gakkō* (college level technical schools), directing them to exert every effort to place the book before the public. The Cabinet Printing Bureau brought out and marketed successive editions and up to March 1943, the last date for which publication figures on this book are obtainable, had sold approximately 1,900,000. In that same period 28,300 reprints by private presses had been sold and approximately 51,200 reproductions of the *Kokutai no Hongi* had appeared in the body of other books. Portions of the text appeared in the textbooks of the Middle School and *seinen gakkō* (youth or continuation schools). It was used both as a textbook and as supplementary reading in the *kōtō gakkō* and *semmon gakkō.* Teaching staffs were compelled to form self-study groups to read and discuss the material contained in the *Kokutai no Hongi.* It was

[2]The Ministry of Education official statistics.

constantly referred to in public speeches and was quoted in the ceremonies of national holidays and school assemblies.

It is perhaps not surprising, when the nature of the book is considered, that despite this impressive total of distributed copies it was virtually impossible to locate one in Japan after the surrender. More surprising, in view of the immense circulation and the avowed objective of the volume, "to cultivate and awaken national sentiment and consciousness," was the extreme difficulty of the text. In the first two years after publication, from July 25, 1937, to August 20, 1939, one of the best known commentaries on the *Kokutai no Hongi*, that of Miura Tōsaku, published in Tokyo by the Tōyō Tosho Kabushiki Kaisha, went through five editions and ninety-three printings. What made it so difficult? Can a book which obviously presented great difficulties to the educated native Japanese be adequately translated for an Occidental reader? Is it possible to understand the *Kokutai no Hongi* without a thorough knowledge of the culture which produced the book?

The most immediate difficulty in understanding the *Kokutai no Hongi* arises from the language in which it was originally written. Japanese is possibly the most difficult written language in common use today. The text of the *Kokutai no Hongi* was admittedly one of the most difficult forms of written Japanese. Because some knowledge of the construction of the language is necessary if certain portions of the volume are to be understood, a brief description may be useful.

Ancient Japanese apparently had no writing system or literature. When Chinese culture was introduced to Japan first via the Korean Peninsula, in the first millennium of the Christian era, the invention of writing was one of the most interesting imports. Chinese was written with ideographs or symbols which stood for meaning, not sounds, but which could be read with the pronunciation used in any of several dialects. It was possible, therefore, for Japanese scholars to use the Chinese ideograph or character for the meaning of a Japanese word and read it either with the pronunciation of the Japanese word or with the Japanese rendition of the Chinese word. Unfortunately, however, Japanese is a highly inflected language requiring word endings for which the Chinese system, evolved for the Chinese language which does not have these inflections, made no provision. In addition there were many words and proper names in the Japanese spoken language which had no counterpart in the Chinese, so that no ideograph existed. To supply this deficiency a system of phonetic syllabary (*kana*) was evolved, by which the words and parts of words for which there was no Chinese ideograph might be reproduced phonetically. Such a hybrid system was bad when it was adopted. It became worse as the nation and the language progressed. Today the writing system can only be counted one of Japan's major tragedies.

Historically the spoken and written languages have been so different as virtually to constitute different languages. Modern Japanese is written in three basic styles: vernacular (*kōgotai*); literary (*bungotai*); and epistolary (*sōrōbun*). A Japanized form of Chinese (*kambun*) roughly corresponding to Latin in English, is occasionally seen, and various sub-styles, such as legal forms, are also used, though the tendency is to bring the written and spoken language closer together. The basic styles are quite dissimilar and are sometimes unintelligible to the reader who has not studied a particular style. Japanese is written in at least five different levels of politeness, determined by the relative social positions of the persons involved and characterized by the extensive use of honorific titles and verbs in the higher levels of politeness. It is written in any of three directions: vertically from top to bottom and from right to left being the most common, but horizontally in both directions also being used. Considered functionally it is written with three different types of symbols: ideographs (*kanji*); "sidewriting" or phonetic transcription of the pronunciation of the ideograph (*furigana*); and phonetic writing (including *kana,* which are used in *furigana;* *romaji;* Braille; etc.)

There are at least one hundred and six different forms of *kanji* or ideographs historically known and the educated Japanese must be able to read three common ones: block or printed form (*kaisho*); modified printed form used in handwriting (*gyōsho*); and cursive or "grass writing" (*sōsho*). Formal or "seal writing" (*reisho*) is seen in old documents, signatures, and artistic works, though only literary students at the university would be likely to study it systematically. The last two forms are not recognizable in general from a knowledge of the former and must be learned separately. In addition many ideographs have abbreviated forms (*ryakuji*) which are commonly used and which are often not recognizable from a knowledge of the full form (*honji*).

There are six basic types of phonetic writing used in Japanese: the syllabary (*kana*); Latinized Japanese (*romaji*); Braille; Japanese shorthand; International Phonetic Alphabet; and Japanese phonetic alphabets such as *Meishō Moji*. By far the most important of these, and the only one directly applicable to the *Kokutai no Hongi*, is the phonetic syllabary or *kana*. Kana is written in four basic ways: printed or block form (*katakana*); cursive form (*hiragana*); a rarer poetic form (*hentaigana*); and a primitive form in which Chinese characters stand not for meaning but for sound (*manyōgana*), seldom used today. There are at least fifteen known systems of writing Japanese phonetically with the Latin letters, but the only two with any currency are the Japan System (*Nihonsiki Romazi*) and a modified form of the Hepburn System known as the Standard System (*Hyōjunshiki Romaji*). Two systems of Braille, one based on an alphabet and the other on a syllabary; five systems of shorthand (*Nakane, Tagusari, Kumazaki, Mōri,* and *Kana*); and an extended number of phonetic alphabets complete the list.

Symbols used as reading aids, including sidewriting which really consists of running footnotes written alongside ideographs in the text, are of three types: phonetic readings given so the character may be recognized by sound (*furigana*); the quite rare use of a simpler ideograph (*furikanji*); and a notation which supplies postpositions and verb endings (*okurigana*) and other grammatical aids for the reading of Japanized Chinese (*kutōten*).

When it is realized that a sixth grade elementary school student is required to know approximately 1300 ideographs; the daily newspaper, unless artificially restricted, uses about 4500; the educated man recognizes 7000; and the scholar claims 20,000 of the more than 50,000 Chinese characters, some idea of the difficulty of the writing system may be appreciated. It should be pointed out, however, that the frequency of these ideographs vary as greatly as do words in an Occidental language and that of the 4500 in a newspaper, about 500 will constitute 70% of the running text, exclusive of *kana*. Mere recognition of these characters is difficult enough, since the ideographs range in complexity from ones having a single brush stroke to ones with a maximum of about forty-five strokes. But ability to read necessitates the further knowledge of the ideograph's phonetic reading, which sometimes runs as high as eighty variations for a single character.

There are three basic types of readings for most of the characters, each of which may be modified by euphonic changes: Japanese reading (*kunyomi*); Chinese reading (*onyomi*), giving the sound of the Japanese rendition of the characteristic Chinese pronunciation of the Chinese word during one of three historical periods (Go-on, Kan-on, and Tō-on); and weird reading (*atejiyomi*), giving a sound of some word wholly different from the ideograph, usually that of another and more common ideograph, a common Japanese synonym, or a Japanese rendition of a foreign loan word. Even *kana* readings are not without difficulty, despite the fact that *kana* are generally considered phonetic since there are a considerable number of traditional and non-phonetic combinations which must be learned.

The language of the *Kokutai no Hongi* very nearly achieves the distinction of suffering from the cumulative difficulties of all these systems. Its basic manuscript, exclusive of quotations from other writings, is written in a mixture of ideograph and phonetic syllabary known as *kanamajiri*. With the exception of horizontal writing, the crude levels of politeness in speech, and the less formal styles of phonetic script (*romaji,* Braille, shorthand, and phonetic alphabet), either the basic text or reference material directly quoted contain many of the above mentioned styles, types of characters, phonetic syllabaries, sidewriting, readings, and honorifics.

The almost sacred status of any official writing about the *kokutai* or national entity has resulted in a level of politeness, formality of style, and extreme use of honorifics which removes the language from the normal contact of most Japanese. Appendix II gives alternate forms for the words for Emperor, Country, and People used in the *Kokutai no Hongi*. The mixed authorship has introduced a puzzling fluctuation in literary style. The constant use of ideological terms which have acquired hazy and unsavory connotations from their political associations makes many passages unintelligible or at least ambiguous even to learned Japanese. The term *kokutai* used in the title is an example. It has usually been officially translated as "national polity" and has acquired as powerful a symbolism in Japanese nationalism as the word "Cross" has in Christianity. It has here been rendered "national entity" in an attempt to reduce it to its unemotional original meaning. Two terms, *Dai Tōa Sensō* (Greater East Asia War) and *hakkō ichiu* (the whole world under one roof) acquired such perverted connotations through the propaganda of the militarists and became such inflammatory symbols for the Japanese people that their use had to be prohibited by the Supreme Commander for the Allied Powers.

Beyond the language difficulties of understanding the *Kokutai no Hongi* there is the tremendous difficulty of understanding the cultural background which produced the volume. The Orientalist who would have a technical knowledge of the book will, of course, prefer to consult the original text and to study the Japanese commentaries. In order to supply the minimum necessary frame of reference in English for the student of politics, modern history, and comparative education who is unequipped with the requisite linguistic and contextual tools, some explanation is clearly necessary. Too extensive footnoting would make the basic text unwieldy and less readable, and would tend to become a somewhat indifferent Occidental commentary roughly paralleling the Japanese. A graded system of reference seemed desirable and was adopted.

For the casual reader very brief footnotes explaining some of the sections most likely to be puzzling to the Occidental reader have been inserted. All footnotes and the appendices at the close of the volume are editorial additions and are not parts of the original Japanese text. In the body of the text dates given in parenthesis are also editorial additions. Dates following an Emperor's name refer to his reign and not his life-span. All dates until the end of the fourth century of the Christian era, and some thereafter, are traditional rather than historical and in some cases are subject to considerable skepticism. Where Japanese authorities differed, the dates given in the standard Japanese chronology, *Mohan Saishin Sekai Nempyō* (Chronological Table of the Historical Events of the World; Tokyo: Sanseidō, 1939), have been used. Quotations of any length have been indented as an aid to the reader, even where the fact that it is a quotation was not indicated in the Japanese text. Short quotations are suitably marked by punctuation.

All Japanese words, with the exception of proper names and some words which have become accepted additions to the English language, have been italicized, and where their meaning is not clear from context have been translated. Japanese proper names have been written in the traditional order with the surname preceding the given name. Where the old form of the names is used with the particle *no* coming between the two names, as for example in the case of Susano-o no Mikoto, the name is read "the Mikoto of Susano-o." The title of *Mikoto* may be unfamiliar to the reader without a fair knowledge of Japanese so that although it means "His Augustness" it has occasionally been translated and repeated in the Japanese even at the risk of tautology, as in "His Augustness

Susano-o no Mikoto." Some of the mythological names, where their internal meaning has bearing on the story, have been translated as well as reproduced in the Japanese form. Chinese names which are commonly known by the English-speaking lay public, such as Laô-tzŭ, have been given with the Chinese pronunciation, but Chinese names which are better known in their Japanese equivalent or are not commonly known, such as Dōsen, are given in the Japanese form.

Occasional examples of tautology occur when the translation is deliberately rendered in somewhat unwieldy English in an attempt to reproduce some of the flavor of the original Japanese style. Even with this concession the English text has a much more precise and less ambiguous feeling than the original. Since number and gender are nonexistent in Japanese the translated text has had to insert information not existing in the original in order to make it intelligible in English. An example is the word *Kōso* which can be rendered "Imperial Ancestor, or Ancestress," or "Imperial Founder, or Founders." In the *Kokutai no Hongi* it usually refers to the Sun Goddess, Amaterasu Ohmikami, and not to the first Emperor Jimmu, founder of the Empire. Capitalization of such words as "Government," "Empire," "Nation," and "People" has been used to indicate a particular significance of the word, as "Government" when it means the administrative organ of the State and "government" when simple administration is intended. The terms "Way" used in the technical ethical sense, and "We" or "Our" used by the Emperor when referring to himself, are further examples.

The *romaji* used in the translation is a modification of the Hepburn System (the so-called *Hyōjunshiki Romaji*), with the exception that *ō* is written as *Oh* when coming at the beginning of a proper noun, as in *Ohmikami*. In order to distinguish between *O-he* and *Oh-e,* for example, a hyphen is inserted to separate *Oh* from the vowel which follows it. Names and words are spelled according to their accepted pronunciation in the Tokyo dialect and not as written in *kana,* as for example *Kammu* rather than *Kwammu.* An exception is made in the rare cases where the reading in *furigana* is given beside a difficult proper name in the Ministry of Education first edition. The reading given by Miura Tōsaku in his commentary was adopted when no official reading was given and authorities differed. The famous anthology of verse, "A Collection of Ten Thousand Leaves," which is referred to frequently in the *Kokutai no Hongi* is romanized as *Mannyōshū* (*Man-nyō-shū*) and not as *Manyōshū* or *Man-yōshū* (*Man-yō-shū*), in order to indicate the orthodox pronunciation. The orthodox reading is given in parenthesis in cases where it differs so much as to impose a difficulty in looking up the word in standard references.

The first portions of the *Kokutai no Hongi* are concerned with the familiar mythological origins of the Japanese nation. Since the concept of unswerving loyalty to an unbroken and eternal line of Emperors, one of the basic tenets of Japanese political philosophy since Meiji, is drawn from these ancient folk tales their content involves more than literary interest. A few words on the early records and mythological era may be of some assistance in following the argument in the first book of the *Kokutai no Hongi*.

Ancient Japan had no known writing system and it was not until approximately A.D. 285[3] that Chinese writing and learning was introduced from Korea. Of the many writings which presumably must have been produced in the following centuries, no document has survived which was actually compiled before the early eighth century. The oldest written records today extant are the *Kojiki* (Records of Ancient Matters) which was compiled by Oh-no-Yasumaro from oral sources in the fifth year of the Wadō era of the Empress Gemmyō (A.D. 712) and the *Nihon-shoki* (or *Nihongi*, Chronicles of Japan) compiled by Prince Toneri, third son of Emperor Temmu, assisted by Oh-no-Yasumaro, in the fourth year of the Yōrō era of the Empress Genshō (A.D. 720). With the exception of extremely fragmentary references to Japan in the literature of other Oriental nations and a few isolated archeo-

[3]Traditional date. Usually given as 405 in Occidental writings.

logical evidences, Japanese history until that age is entirely based on these two records. Both have been translated into English. The translations of short quotations in the text of the *Kokutai no Hongi* have been done by the translator in conformity with other quoted materials. For the convenience of the reader who may wish to read the quotation in its full context, footnotes have been appended referring to the following editions of Chamberlain's and Aston's standard translations:

Basil Hall Chamberlain, trans., *Kojiki, or Records of Ancient Matters*. Transactions of the Asiatic Society of Japan, Vol. X, Supplement, 1882. Reprinted 1906.

William George Aston, trans., *Nihongi: Chronicles of Japan from the Earliest Times to A.D. 697*, 2 vols. Supplement I of the Transactions and Proceedings of the Japan Society of London, 1896.

The legend of the creation of Japan, as contained in these two ancient documents, begins with the universe in a misty chaotic mass containing certain germs of life. The purer part separated into Heaven and the grosser element settled down and became the Earth, which at first floated in the nebulous mass of the heavens. A reed-like growth was produced and became transformed into a God, and this was followed by a number of other spontaneously created male Gods. The creation of the physical nation begins with two gods, Izanagi no Mikoto (His Augustness the Male-who-invites) and Izanami no Mikoto (Her Augustness the Female-who-invites), who while standing on a floating bridge in Heaven dipped a jeweled spear down into the mists and found the ocean. The brine which dripped from the point of the spear coagulated and formed an island to which they descended and on which they lived. Beginning there their life as husband and wife they created by birth a series of islands, the sea, the rivers, the mountains, and finally the ancestors of trees and herbs.

In giving birth to a Fire-God, Izanami was severely burned, died, went to Yomi the Land of Darkness, and began to dissolve. She commanded her mate, Izanami, not to look but he disobeyed and as punishment was pursued by a horrible female deity, until he took courage and drove her off. In purifying himself after this encounter Izanagi washed himself and thus created Amaterasu Ohmikami (The Sun Goddess, or literally Heavenly-Shining-Great-August-Deity) from his left eye; the Moon God, Tsuki-yomi, from his right eye; a dwarfed leech-child that they abandoned; and finally from his nose, the Storm God, Susano-o no Mikoto (Swift-Impetuous-Male-August-Deity). The Sun Goddess, Amaterasu, was sent to Heaven to reign and her younger brother Tsuki-yomi, the Moon God, followed to help govern the heavens.

In due course Susano-o, the Storm God went to Heaven and so terrified his sister the Sun Goddess Amaterasu that she shut herself up in a cave and the universe became dark. At this point the "eight hundred myriads of Deities" assembled and made plans to entice her out. They made an eight-hand metal mirror of *Yata* and a curved string of five hundred jewels of *Yasakani* as placatory offerings. Then one of the older Goddesses did an absurd and obscene dance which made the assembled Gods laugh. Amaterasu, curious at the gaiety when the darkness should have caused gloom, peeped out to see what was transpiring. She was pulled out of the cave by a strong God and prevailed upon to return to the open Heavens. The Storm God, Susano-o, cruel and fierce, was banished to a Nether-Land but on his way went to Korea and then to the region of Izumo on the Sea of Japan where he killed an eight headed serpent and found the sacred sword of *Kusanagi* (*Murakumo*) in its tail. These three Imperial Treasures (the sword for justice, the jewels for mercy, and the mirror for truth) were later given by the Sun Goddess to her grandson Ninigi no Mikoto (His Augustness the Prosperity-Man) on the occasion of his descent to Earth, and have been handed down from Emperor to Emperor to the present time.

Ninigi, the grandson of the Sun Goddess was sent to Earth to rule guided by a Divine Oracle stated by Amaterasu:

The Luxuriant Land of Reed Plains is the country which our descendants are to govern as monarchs. Go forth, therefore, Ye Imperial Grandson, and rule over it! May Ye fare well. Our Imperial lineage shall continue unbroken and prosperous, co-eternal with heaven and earth.[4]

Prior to his descent, however, Ninigi sent two lesser Gods to Earth to deliver this Oracle to Ohkuninushi no Kami (Deity-Master-of-Great-Land), most powerful of the eighty-one sons, probably a son-in-law, of Susano-o, the obstreperous younger brother of the Sun Goddess. Ohkuninushi and his son Kotoshironushi no Kami, rulers of Izumo, or the southwestern part of the main Japanese island of Honshu, agreed to the sovereignty of the chosen Grandson of the Sun Goddess and had a beautiful palace built for them in recompense. Reassured, Ninigi then assumed his duties of ruling the land after descending to Earth on Mount Takachiho in what is the modern prefecture of Miyazaki in eastern Kyushu. The instrument of this unifying rule was the Great-Grandson of Ninigi, and hence the fifth generation descendant of the Sun Goddess Amaterasu: Jimmu, the Founder and First Emperor of Japan. He is credited with subjugating all the local chiefs, presumably descendants of Susano-o, in the Yamato region, the modern Nara prefecture in central Honshu. The Empire is traditionally dated from his coronation at the Kashiwara Palace in 660 B.C. The confusing relationships between the Gods mentioned in the *Kokutai no Hongi* may be clarified by Appendix I, an abridged genealogy of the pertinent Deities, stripped of their honorific titles for simplicity.

The *Kokutai no Hongi* cannot be understood without some knowledge of the common religions of Japan. There are four: Christianity, Confucianism, Buddhism, and Shinto.

Christianity is the most recently established and to date the least influential of the four. Between 1549, when the great Jesuit

---

[4]Official translation. Compare with page 63 of text.

Francis Xavier landed at Kagoshima, and 1638 when the Shimabara Rebellion was suppressed, the Roman Catholic Church established missions, made converts and exerted some force in the social
and political life of Japan. A series of unfortunate incidents caused
Nobunaga (A.D. 1534-1582), though previously friendly, to restrict
the foreign missionaries and led Hideyoshi (A.D. 1536-1598) to
expel them from the country. The Shimabara Rebellion of 1637
linked Christianity with political revolt in the minds of the Shoguns
of the early Tokugawa period and brought severe persecution which
apparently stamped out all vestiges of the faith with the exception
of a few isolated clandestine churches near Nagasaki which survived until 1865 when the Roman Catholic Church reëntered Japan.
Protestant missionaries entered Japan after the reopening of the
nation in 1854. They were allowed to enter the ports of Kanagawa,
Nagasaki, and Hakodate and to found missions after 1859. They
opened schools in 1873, finished translating the Holy Bible in 1886,
and secured full religious freedom with the Constitution of 1889.
The Russian Orthodox Church has been established in Japan since
1861 but has had limited membership and influence. The *Kokutai
no Hongi* acknowledges the influence of the small but active religious movement of the Christian Church largely by indirection.
Christianity is often linked with Westernism and individualism in
Japan, and accordingly is the antithesis of the belief in the divine
origin of the Empire and infallibility of the Imperial Line. Hence,
by implication, Christianity is part of the ideological threat to the
ultranationalist Japan which this book advocates. Appendix III
gives the best available official figures for membership in the various religious bodies at the time of the publication of the *Kokutai
no Hongi*.

Confucianism is considered by many Japanese not a religion but
rather a moral philosophy. Being free from ritualistic observances
and only by implication concerned with many of the basic spiritual
concepts of other religions, it has not severely clashed with the great
competing religions of Buddhism and Shinto. Frequently, in fact,

the priests of these religions have been the best known Confucian philosophers, apparently without intellectual conflict or emotional disturbance. It was traditionally introduced into Japan by Wani, envoy to the Emperor Ohjin from the King of Kudara (Paikché) one of the ancient principalities of Korea, in A.D. 285, when Wani brought the *Rongo* (Lun Yü, or Analects) and the *Senjimon* (Ch'ien Tzu Wen, or Thousand Ideographs) as teaching material for Ohjin's son and Crown Prince, Wakiiratsuko. The history of Confucianism in Japan has been divided into four periods: the first producing mainly philological commentaries on the classics and lasting to about A.D. 1298; the second a period of 303 years dating from A.D. 1299 when Nei-issan, a Chinese priest, arrived and began to expound the Sung School; the third the 265 years of the Golden Age of Confucianism under the Tokugawa Shogunate ending in 1867; and the last period that dating from the Meiji Restoration to the present. The *Kokutai no Hongi* is permeated with the ethical principles of Confucianism. Especially adaptable to the system of ultranationalism which this volume expounds, have been those principles of loyalty and filial piety based on the five Confucian relationships of sovereign and subject; father and child; husband and wife; elder and younger brother (or sister); and friends. The greatest single document of Japanese policy, the *Imperial Rescript on Education* issued by Emperor Meiji on October 30, 1890, is about equally an expression of these Confucian concepts and of the Shinto beliefs in the mythological genesis of Japan. It is reproduced in full in Appendix IV.

Buddhism has been the greatest religious force in Japan and also its most powerful intellectual movement. For centuries Buddhism and learning were almost synonymous. Tradition credits the formal founding of Buddhism in Japan to a mission from the King of Kudara in Korea to the Court of Emperor Kimmei in 552, which brought as gifts an image of Buddha and certain of the sacred books. This was followed by a steady flow of Buddhist priests, nuns, artisans, and craftsmen who introduced not only the philosophies of Indian and Chinese Buddhism but also the culture of continental Asia.

Buddhism as a religious philosophy had begun during the forty-five years of the wandering ministry of Siddhārtha, known as Śakyamuni or the Gautama Buddha (circa B.C. 560-480)[5] in India. His philosophy, which denied the elaborate rites and mysticism then common in the Brahman Religion, is most succinctly stated in the Sermon of Benares and is known as the Three Law Seals[6] (Jap. *Sambōin,* Sanskrit Trividyā); The Four Noble Truths (Jap. *Shitai,* Sanskrit Catuāri Āryāsatyāni); and The Noble Eightfold Path (Jap. *Hachi Shōdō,* Sanskrit Āryāstānga Mārga). He believed in the impermanence of all existence, in the universality of human suffering, and in the nonexistence or nonreality of human ego. The Gautama Buddha's teachings were modified markedly by his followers, quickly reassuming much of the ceremony he despised, and acquiring the mysticism which marked Hinduism. Voluminous writings by the early religious leaders were canonized in four great synods, Rajagriha, Vaisālī, Pātaliputra, and Jalandhara. Two streams of Buddhism were produced, Hīnayāna and Mahāyāna. Hīnayāna Buddhism (Lesser Vehicle) under the patronage of King Asoka (Priyadarsin) about B.C. 240 spread widely over Southern Asia and survives today as "Southern Buddhism" in South East Asia. Mahāyāna Buddhism (Greater Vehicle) is traditionally considered to have been founded by Asvaghosha, a converted Brahman who wandered widely through India and finally settled in Benares (sometime between B.C. 100 and A.D. 300). The writings of Asvaghosha, many of which probably were written by other priests but were attributed to him, together with those of Nāgārjuna became the basis of the division of Mahāyāna, or "Northern Buddhism," into sects. Asanga, one of the great Mahāyāna writers of the

---

[5]See August Karl Reischauer, *Studies in Japanese Buddhism* (New York: The Macmillan Co., 1917), p. 22. The *Mohan Saishin Sekai Nempyō* gives B.C. 557-477, based on Max Mueller's opinions. Many other dates have been advanced.

[6]Not specifically mentioned in the Sermon of Benares.

V Century A.D. laid the foundation for syncretism and the absorption of competing religions by the process of identification of their gods with deities in the expanding Buddhist pantheon.

Mahāyāna Buddhism went from India into Persia, north to the Black Sea, crossed Turkestan and settled in China about A.D. 147. Chinese Buddhism was augmented by direct importations from India, as by the arrival in A.D. 520 of Bodhidharma, the founder of the Zen Sect of Contemplative Buddhism. It was influenced by Confucianism and Taoism from indigenous Chinese philosophies and in VII Century A.D. by the reimportation of a debased form of Buddhism, the Lamaism of Tibet and Mongolia, which originally had been exported to those regions from China itself. Flowing into Korea, both directly from China and via Mongolia, Mahāyāna Buddhism was introduced into Japan and so stirred the political and intellectual leaders of that empire that Chinese priests were invited to Japan and Japanese scholars went to China to study. In the reign of Empress Suiko (A.D. 593-628) the actual ruler, Prince Shōtoku, gave to Japanese Buddhism the same protection and patronage that King Asoka had Hīnayāna or Southern Buddhism in India. After his death divergent sects began to appear with the increased exchange of scholars between China and Japan.

The so-called "Six Sects of the Southern Capital" (Nara) included the Sanron Sect introduced from China by Ekan (Ekwan) in A.D. 625; the Jōjitsu Sect also introduced by Ekan in 625; the Hossō Sect brought from China by Dōshō sometime between A.D. 625 and 653; the Kusha Sect brought from China by Chitsu and Chitatsu in A.D. 658; the Kegon Sect brought from China by Dōsen, a Chinese priest, in A.D. 736, and Bodhisena, an Indian priest, but usually credited to the Korean priest Jingō (Shinshō) who arrived circa A.D. 740 to lecture on the Avatamsaka-Sutra; and the Ritsu Sect introduced from China in A.D. 754 by Ganjin, a Chinese priest.

Two of the most powerful and influential sects today existing are known as the Heian or Kyoto Sects. These were the Tendai

Sect introduced into Japan from China by the Japanese priest Dengyō Daishi (Saichō) in A.D. 805 when he returned from study of the Chinese Sect at Mt. T'ien-t'ai; and the Shingon Sect founded by Kōbō Daishi (Kūkai) upon his return from China in A.D. 807. These two sects, while based on direct importation of doctrine from China, are really Japanese in nature. Kōbō Daishi (A.D. 774-835), a truly remarkable personality credited by tradition with the invention of *kana* or phonetic syllabary and the establishment of the Sōgei Shuchiin, first public school for the masses, accomplished the brilliant tour de force of identifying the gods in the Shinto pantheon with those in the Buddhist, thus enabling the loyal Japanese to continue their classic reverence for the mythological creators of the nation and at the same time accept Buddhism. This compromise of the conflicting elements of Buddhism and Shinto, also in part due to the priests, Gyōgi and Saichō, was later known as Ryōbu Shintō (Double Aspect Shinto).

In the twelfth century A.D. there occurred a widespread religious movement which was somewhat similar to the Christian Reformation. In the process six "Sects of the Great Awakening" were established. Four were Amida Sects which believed that salvation could only come by faith in the name of Amida Butsu. These made repetition of the prayer *Namu Amida Butsu* (I adore Thee, Thou Buddha of Eternal Life) a major part of their liturgy. The Ji Sect, a relatively unimportant and small organization founded by Ippen Shōnin in A.D. 1276, and the Yūzū Nembutsu Sect founded by Ryōnin, a Tendai priest, in A.D. 1126 were of this type. Two other Amida sects are usually known as the "Pure Land Sects" because their doctrine includes a concept of a Paradise or Pure Land. The Jōdo Sect was founded in A.D. 1175 by Hōnen Shōnin, and the very powerful Shin Sect (or more properly Jōdo Shinshū) was founded by Hōnen's greatest disciple, Shinran Shōnin, in A.D. 1224.

The two remaining sects of this great movement were the Nichiren Sect founded in A.D. 1253 by Nichiren Shōnin, who had studied Shingon, Tendai, and openly hated the Amida sects, with

a doctrine of return to the original teachings of the Gautama
Buddha; and the mystical and militaristic Zen sect. This latter was
introduced from China by Eisai in A.D. 1191 in the form of a
subsect Rinzai and by Dōgen in the form of the subsect Sōtō, and
today has a third subsect Ohbaku. It is a contemplative religion
which seeks "salvation by meditation and divine emptiness." Because of the powerful hold which it has held over the military
classes of Japan, Zen is the form of Buddhism which has most
affected Japanese ultranationalist philosophy. It is implicit in many
of the concepts of self-denial and sacrifice for the Imperial Family
which are basic to the theme of the *Kokutai no Hongi*. Appendix
III gives the present Buddhist Sects in Japan with their pre-war
following.

The ancient indigenous religion of Japan was Shinto (Shintō),
although the term itself is of relatively modern origin, introduced
to differentiate between Buddhism and Kami Nagara. It was a
primitive animistic religion with elements of ancestor worship. In
its earliest known form natural objects such as mountains, groves
of trees, rocks, waterfalls and rivers, and especially trees served
as sanctuaries, but man-made shrines were erected long before
historic time. Worship consisted of festivals, largely connected with
agricultural seasons and the act of procreation. A priesthood composed of Nakatomi (Ritualists), Imibe (Abstainers), Urabe (Di-
viners), and Sarume (Musicians and Dancers) developed. The Ritualists read *norito* or poetic prayers, while the Abstainers conducted
ceremonies of purification to ward off pollution from unclean objects
and acts. Purification from such things as sickness, sexual contact,
excrement, and anything involving blood (such as menstruation)
was accomplished by burning in fire, casting away into running
water, cleansing with salt, and by transference of the contamination
to some inanimate object, usually a doll. These rites have come
down in three forms to the present day: *harai* (exorcism) with the
waving of an *ohnusa* or wand in the form of a branch; *misogi*
(cleansing) with sprinkling of salt or water and the washing of

hands; and *imi* (abstention) with the priesthood practicing rituals involving the avoidance of contact with unclean things.

The history of Shinto in Japan is both vague and complex. Three great events, however, stand out. These were the fusion with Confucianism, the rise of Ryōbu Shintō, and the rise of Kokka Shintō.

The fusion of Shinto with Confucianism took place prior to recorded history. It strengthened and possibly created the element of ancestor worship which exists in the traditional Japanese worship of *kami* (Gods) and belief in the divine origin of the Imperial Family, the Nation, and the People. What the actual contribution of Confucianism to Japanese mythology may have been is, of course, only speculative since it occurred generations before the compilation of the *Kojiki* and the *Nihongi*. But there exists a suspicious similarity between some of the presumably indigenous folk-tales of Japanese mythology and the ancient beliefs of China.

The second great event is amply documented. It was the syncretism of Buddhism and Shinto through the process of establishing the identity of the gods of one religion in the pantheon of the other. Two Buddhist sects contributed to this concept. The Tendai Sect founded by Dengyō Daishi (A.D. 767-822) formulated the philosophy known as Sannō Ichi-jitsu Shintō (Mountain-King-One-Reality-Shinto) establishing an absolute Buddha and under this a multitude of manifest Buddhas who appeared from time to time in the form of various gods and goddesses of other religions. The Shingon Sect founded by Kōbō Daishi (A.D. 774-835) helped to formulate the school of thought known as Ryōbu Shintō (Double Aspect Shinto) which has already been mentioned.

The third of the great stages in the development of modern Shinto was the creation of Kokka Shintō or Jinja Shintō (State or Shrine Shinto), the official national cult of Japan after 1867. This State Shinto was officially considered to be a "nonreligious official cult" and was so established by a tortuous religious and legal process. By thus drawing the line between the religion and the official cult it was possible to compel outward acceptance of State Shinto with all its political implications without obviously violating the freedom of religious belief provided for in the national Constitution and without antagonizing the powerful Buddhist Church. Even the Roman Catholic Church on May 25, 1936, by the Sacred Congregation of Propaganda Fide, found it expedient and technically possible to accept the State Rites as veneration of departed persons and not the worship of false gods.

The philosophy of State Shinto drew heavily upon the writings of the opponents of Ryōbu Shintō. This opposition was led originally by Urabe Kanetomo (A.D. 1435-1511), one of the creators of Yui-ichi Shintō (Only-one Shinto), and later by the leaders of the reform movement known as Fukko Shintō (Renaissance or Revival of Ancient Learning Shinto). Fukko Shintō was pioneered by Kada Azumamaro (A.D. 1669-1736) but is usually associated with its greatest writers, Moto-ori Norinaga (A.D. 1730-1801) and Hirata Atsutane (A.D. 1776-1843). This form of Shinto practically substituted the *Kojiki* and the *Nihongi* for the scriptural writings of all faiths and placed Amaterasu Ohmikami, the Sun Goddess, as the Founder of the Nation, First Ancestor of the Imperial Family, and Chief Deity of the Pantheon of Japanese *Kami*. Fukko Shintō, frequently called Pure Shinto, thus provided the basis for quasi-religious fervor and loyalty to the concept of an Imperial line destined to rule eternally and of a Nation and People which by their divine origin possessed a certain racial superiority and privilege. It was clearly a powerful instrument for ultranationalism.

In addition to the State Shinto there have been two other forms of Shinto in Japan, both openly religious in character. One is the survival of certain folk customs in connection with the home and village shrines. The other is Kyōha Shintō (Sect Shinto) which consists of thirteen legally recognized religious bodies,[7] all varying

---

[7]The SCAP Directive dated October 4, 1945, entitled, "Removal of Restrictions on Political, Civil, and Religious Liberties," abrogated the Religious Bodies Law (No. 77 of 1939) and permitted the formation of additional sects, many of which have sprung up since that time.

somewhat in their ritualistic observances and in their doctrines but all based on the mythology and writings recognized by State Shinto. Until the surrender of Japan at the end of World War II it was obligatory for all Japanese to profess to believe in the national cult of State Shinto, but prior to the War less than eighteen million, or approximately one quarter of the population, were affiliated with Sect Shinto. These thirteen religious sects with their pre-war statistics are given in Appendix III.

The *Kokutai no Hongi* is primarily an educational book written for educators. It presupposes a background knowledge of the educational system and is full of allusions which cannot be understood without this background. A few brief notes on the historical development of the system which was in existence in Japan at the time of the writing of the *Kokutai no Hongi* may aid the casual reader.

Like all primitive countries, ancient Japan transmitted its accumulated knowledge from generation to generation by informal family and clan teaching. Traditionally, formal education was introduced at the time of the importation of Chinese ideographs from Korea about A.D. 285 by Wani, tutor of Prince Wakiiratsuko. Court schools modeled after the Chinese, and some formal governmental schools probably existed before A.D. 664 when the Emperor Tenchi appointed a Korean, Kishitsu-Shushi, to the position of "superintendent of education." The first specific institution known to exist was a college or school of higher learning which was founded at Ōtsu, near Kyoto, about A.D. 668. Formal governmental education, however, is generally considered to date from the famous *Taihōryo,* a part of the *Taihō-ritsuryō* (Law Code of the Taihō Era), composed of thirty volumes of Imperial edicts and regulations begun in the reign of Emperor Tenchi (A.D. 661-671) and completed in A.D. 701 in the reign of Emperor Mommu (A.D. 697-707). This code provided for a tax-supported central system of schools and a university, but restricted education to the children of civil officials of the higher ranks. Persons who wished to become priests were trained in monasteries and temples.

Early Japanese education and culture reached a peak about the ninth century A.D. in the early part of the Heian Era and then declined. The five hundred years from the beginning of the Kamakura Era (A.D. 1184) to the beginning of the Edo Era (A.D. 1603) constituted the educational dark ages. Learning was kept alive by the private efforts of the priesthood, largely Buddhist. The Edo Era, also known as the period of the Tokugawa Shogunate, was essentially a military feudalism founded upon the military prowess of the three great early leaders, Oda Nobunaga (A.D. 1533-1583), Toyotomi Hideyoshi (A.D. 1536-1598), and Tokugawa Ieyasu (Iyeyasu) (A.D. 1542-1616). After 1615 when Ieyasu fought his last decisive battle against contending clan leaders, the society of Japan was stratified into the official or noble class (*kuge*); warriors (*buke*); farmers (*hyakushō*); townspeople (*chōnin*); and outcastes (*eta* or *hinin*). Below the Imperial Family, which was reduced to an inconsequential puppet position, was the real governmental power, the Shōgun, a sort of Chancellor whose authority stemmed from his position as head of the Tokugawa Clan. This official commanded the support of about two hundred and seventy feudal lords, or *daimyō,* each of whom was in turn supported by warriors or professional swordsmen, *samurai.* Schools were revived and two types predominated. One, restricted to the children of *samurai,* was analogous to the schools of European chivalry and concentrated on such things as the tea ceremony and the warlike arts, especially swordsmanship. The other was the *terakoya* (temple school) where the commoners learned the basic skills of reading, calligraphy, and simple numbers. The basic political policy of this period was that of the "closed-door" by which the Shōgun hoped to exclude all foreign influence. No foreigners, except the Chinese and to a limited degree the Dutch were permitted to enter Japan, and no Japanese was permitted to leave.

A small amount of Occidental learning seeped past the vigilant guard of the Shogunate. The Portuguese, French, and Spanish culture introduced by the early Roman Catholic missionaries almost entirely died. In the early part of the Tokugawa Shogunate it was punishable by death to be found in possession of a foreign book (except Chinese). Later, however, a handful of Dutch scientists, such as Dr. Engelbert Kaempfer who arrived in 1690 and Philipp Franz von Siebold who arrived in 1823, gained limited access to Japan posing as employees of the Dutch East Indies Trading Company. The Dutch were restricted to a small artificial island, Deshima, in Nagasaki. On the annual official visit to the Shōgun at Edo (now called Tokyo) to pay their official respects, however, these scientists were occasionally able to exchange information surreptitiously with some of the more daring scholars of Japan. After 1720 a slightly more liberal attitude was taken toward the importation of limited numbers of scientific works in Dutch, but since no language schools existed and foreign study or the admission of foreign translators was rigidly forbidden, the learning in these books did not spread widely. A few Japanese were permitted to study Dutch in Nagasaki in order to act as official interpreters but their command of the language was poor and their influence slight. In 1860 the Shogunate established an official foreign language school to train interpreters in Dutch, French, German, Russian, and English, and permitted missionaries, often capable scientists and teachers, to enter Japan. Among the outstanding of these early missionaries who did much to form early Meiji education were Dr. G. F. Verbeck, the Dutch-American civil engineer, S. R. Brown, D. C. Greene, and Dr. J. C. Hepburn, creator of modern *romaji* and compiler of the first Japanese-English bilingual dictionary.

On April 6, 1868, Emperor Meiji took the famous "Charter Oath of Five Principles," which contains the statement: "Wisdom and ability should be sought throughout the world for the purpose of promoting the welfare of the Empire."[8] This opened the floodgates to foreign knowledge. Japanese students were sent abroad for study and large numbers of contract teachers and technicians were brought

[8]New official Japanese translation.

from England, the United States, Germany, and France to teach in Japanese schools.

Although the first National Superintendent of Schools, analogous to the present Vice-Minister of Education, was an American, Dr. David Murray, who arrived in August 1873, and the first textbooks were translations of American public school texts, the educational system adopted was a very close copy of the French system. This highly centralized governmental educational structure lent itself to the complete control and facile manipulation which the Meiji Government felt was needed in the critical first years of the Restoration. In January 1871 the national educational system was put in charge of the Mombushō the newly created Department of Education which was later raised to Cabinet rank as the Ministry of Education.

The real beginnings of modern education in Japan date from the Educational Code of 1872. This remarkable plan called for the establishment of eight universities in eight university districts, the formation of 256 middle schools and 53,760 elementary schools. All were to be under federal control and to be supported largely by federal taxation. The distribution of the schools in the eight districts was to be on a rather unimaginative geographical basis which did not recognize adequately the various concentrations of population. Although this projected system was found in practice to be far too ambitious for immediate instrumentation as planned, and although it was modified considerably in details and in time-schedule for adoption, it did provide a farsighted goal which inspired the Japanese people to efforts that were remarkable. This projected system was modified by the Education Decree of September 1879, the University and Lower School Ordinances of March and April 1886, and the Elementary School Decree of October 1890. The highly centralized pattern which had been evolved and in a considerable degree put into operation by 1890 was modified from time to time (especially in 1907, 1917, 1935, 1940, and 1947) but after

1890 the school system of Japan was strikingly similar to what it was in 1937 at the time of the writing of the *Kokutai no Hongi*. The reforms had been of detail rather than of substance.

Compulsory elementary education was advocated in the Code of 1872 and was specifically established through the fourth grade by the Elementary School Decree of 1886 and 1890. In March 1907 the period of compulsory education was raised to six years although it was not actually put into effect until April of the following year. This was in turn raised to eight years by the National School Reform begun in April 1941. Although Japan was actually unable to put into effect nation-wide compulsory education through the eighth grade in the War years, the Ministry of Education on January 20, 1947, announced the extension of compulsory education to nine years, in compliance with the recommendations made by the United States Education Mission to Japan in March 1946. There is no immediate possibility of supplying or enforcing this extended compulsory schooling.)

In the sixty-five years between the writing of the Code of 1872 and the publication of the *Kokutai no Hongi* the Japanese educational system grew to be one of the outstanding structures in the world. Unquestionably the most important cultural event in Japan during those years was the issuing of the *Imperial Rescript on Education* by Emperor Meiji on October 30, 1890. This document has acquired an aura of sacred scripture in Japan and has become the uncontested fountainhead of all social and educational policy and of much of the political thinking. It is reproduced in full in its official English translation in Appendix IV. Acknowledging all authority as coming from the divine origin and unbroken descent of the present Imperial Family, and establishing a code of ethics based on the patriarchal Confucian structure of social obligations, the *Imperial Rescript on Education* is vague enough so that parts may be construed as mere formal phrases in traditional language or as an expression of national destiny. It is repeatedly alluded to or directly quoted in the *Kokutai no Hongi*. By official interpretation, it was possible for militaristic leaders in Japan to convert a relatively innocuous and even rather impressive document into a tool of ultranationalism. The jingoistic perversion of the probable original intent of this Rescript became apparent in 1931. It was intensified in 1937 and culminated in 1941. These interpretations were characterized by a doctrine of total subservience of the individual to the State, by a belief in the divine mission of Japan in East Asia and in the entire world, and by an admiration of and proficiency in the military arts.

The Educational System of Japan in 1937 was directed by a powerful national Ministry of Education, the Mombushō. This Ministry was headed by a Minister of Education holding Cabinet rank who was appointed by the Premier with the consent of the Emperor. The Minister of Education was assisted by a Vice-Minister, a Parliamentary Vice-Minister, a Parliamentary Councilor and a private secretariat. Internal administration of the Ministry was entrusted to the Minister's Secretariat. External control of the school was through orders sent to school officials at the prefectural (Ken) and university level, and through a Division of Superintendents and Inspectors in the Ministry. All official proclamations and directives were passed on by a Legal Inquiry Committee, prototype of numerous subsequent advisory and semiautonomous technical committees temporarily attached to the Ministry.

The Vice-Minister of Education was the highest educational official holding permanent civil service rank and hence was relatively unaffected by changes of the national Cabinet. Under him were eight permanent Bureaus: Higher Education, General Education, Technical Education, School Books, Social Education, Educational Reform (Thought Control), Religion, and Educational Research. The composition and duties of these bureaus, and in fact the bureaus themselves, have been changed from time to time by the frequent and often insignificant reorganizations which have characterized the Ministry in the past and which are even continuing under the supervision of the Occupation authorities. The duties have remained the same: the establishment of over-all policy; the development of curricula; the licensing of teachers; the compilation and publication of textbooks; the direct inspection, supervision, and administration of schools above the elementary level and the indirect supervision of schools of the elementary level through the prefectural educational officials; the conducting of research; the allocation of educational funds; and the supervision of a considerable number of concomitant matters relating to art, science, literature, and religion. Three functions of the Ministry of Education in 1937 might seem somewhat unusual. These were jurisdiction over civil service examinations; supervision of the religious bodies of Japan including financial and legal control of the Shinto shrines, national treasures, and historical monuments; and direction of thought control activities. This latter included both punitive action against persons with thoughts considered officially undesirable, and the creation and dissemination of propaganda for the control of student thought. The *Kokutai no Hongi* is a product of the Bureau of Educational Reform, which was charged with thought control.

The Japanese School System of 1937 was divided into four areas: Elementary Education; Secondary Education; Higher Education; and Special Education.

Elementary Education consisted of three levels: the Kindergartens (*yōchien*) which were noncompulsory pre-school institutions found mainly in the metropolitan areas; the Ordinary Elementary Schools (*jinjō shō gakkō*) which were six-year compulsory tax-supported schools, ostensibly under local direction but actually under the control of the prefectural educational authorities and the Higher Elementary Schools (*kōtō shō gakkō*) which were two or three year terminal courses, noncompulsory, designed for students not going on to the Middle School. The Ordinary Elementary Schools enrolled approximately 75% of all students enrolled at all levels and were internationally famous because they had a 99.7% average attendance of all students of compulsory school age. Approximately 40% of the time devoted to all instruction in these schools was given to learning the written language. The second most important subject was arithmetic, and the third, occupying only about 8% of the time, was Japanese Ethics (*shūshin*), which originally was a course in social customs and citizenship but which by 1937 had become a vehicle for ultranationalistic and militaristic propaganda.

Secondary Education was provided through three units, roughly parallel in age level but differing widely in curricula. The traditional Boys Middle School (*chū gakkō*) was a non-compulsory, tax-supported basic preparatory school of four to five years duration designed for boys who intended to enter the university or who wished a cultural rather than a vocational terminal course. Graduation did not lead directly to the university but to a higher preparatory school (*kōtō gakkō*) which by its admission requirements virtually controlled admission to the university. In 1937 the Boys Middle School was divided into two levels, the first two years offering a more intensive continuation of the elementary school subjects together with a limited number of new subjects, such as English, and the last three years offering a required basic curriculum and certain electives. The Girls Middle School (*kōtō jo gakkō*), sometimes called the Girls Higher School, was a feminized counterpart. A third category of secondary schools, known as Special Schools (*jitsugyō gakkō*) included trade, technical, vocational, commercial, continuation, and schools for the handicapped. Included in this group were some schools, such as for the training of police, foresters, merchant marine petty officers, and fishermen, which were under the authority of other Ministries than the Ministry of Education. The most important in size and influence of all special schools was the Youth School (*seinen gakkō*), sometimes classed as an elementary school because it offered one to seven-year part-time continuation studies for graduates of the elementary school and in its lower grades paralleled the Higher Elementary School. The Youth School was made the tool of the military clique shortly after its formation in 1935 and by 1941 was openly an instrument for the circulation of propaganda.

Higher education in 1937 was divided among four institutions.

The Boys Higher School (*kōtō gakkō*) was a three-year post-secondary preparatory course leading to admission to the university. The name was also given to a seven-year school which was really a *kōtō gakkō* and *chū gakkō* combined. The final three years were approximately equivalent to the junior college in the American system. Because virtually every student admitted to one of these schools was assured of entrance to some university, although only a small percentage of the original applicants would be privileged to enter the highly desirable Imperial Universities, admission to the *kōtō gakkō* was both selective and competitive. The University (*daigaku*) was the highest level of Japanese education and was composed of one or more Faculties offering specialized three to five-year courses in the various professional areas and in the disciplines of the arts and sciences. The University resembled French, Italian, or Latin-American universities in organization more than it did American or British. Electives were held to a minimum. Colleges or Technical Institutes (*semmon gakkō*) were higher educational institutions not necessarily requiring graduation from the Boys Higher School for entrance and not having the social or academic standing of a university. They offered three to five-year terminal courses in technical fields. The fourth type of higher educational institution was the Normal School, divided into two levels. The common Normal School (*shihan gakkō*) offered a five-year course preparatory to becoming a teacher in the elementary schools. The Higher Normal School for Men and for Women (*kōtō shihan gakkō* and *joshi kōtō shihan gakkō*) were four-year training courses for teachers in the secondary schools. The University alone of all the major Japanese institutions had any real measure of autonomy and the consequent intellectual freedom enjoyed before and even during the War made of it a center of the rather limited form of liberalism which survived the militaristic domination of Japan.

On March 9, 1940, the Ministry of Education announced the completion of a plan of sweeping reforms of the school system which was to be initiated with the beginning of the following academic year in April 1941. This plan, known as the National School Reform, reflected the growing sense of nationalism in Japan. The old elementary schools of *shō gakkō* and *kōtō shō gakkō* were replaced by a National School (*kokumin gakkō*) of eight years, divided into an upper cycle of two years and a lower cycle of six. The curriculum, although it did not undergo radical changes in subjects and hours, actually was markedly changed by a reorientation of the subjects toward extreme nationalism. Vocational training and physical education received increased emphasis. The teaching staff, which in Japan has traditionally been a respected though somewhat conformist professional group, was reduced to the position of mouthpiece for official propaganda. Military officers were placed in key positions and held superior jurisdiction over the students.

All mass information media had been increasingly subjected to governmental control before 1937 and by the time of the publication of the *Kokutai no Hongi* had ceased to have any real freedom. The Ministry of Education controlled the production and use of all textbooks through the elementary schools and sanctioned those in the secondary and higher schools. Through the Cabinet Board of Information the Ministry controlled all radio programs used for educational purposes. It controlled the Central Film Education Association which had the monopoly on all films used in schools. It controlled the All-Japan Gramophone Corporation which held the monopoly on phonograph records used in schools. The Ministry of Education with the Japanese copy of the French educational system proved to be an instrument through which a Cabinet Minister and eight Bureau Chiefs could control 36% of the total population, those children below the maximum age of compulsory education. The *Kokutai no Hongi* was the propaganda line of this control. This volume had a profound influence on the educational system, through examination questions, through reference material for teachers, through the training programs for student teachers, and through official policy instructions for practicing teachers.

Reading the *Kokutai no Hongi* in retrospect almost inevitably leads to two questions. What has the Occupation done to the volume and to the political and social philosophy which created it? And how have the Japanese reacted to the volume and its expressed philosophy in the light of their military defeat and Allied punitive action? To answer in any detail would be to write the definitive history of the Occupation. This is manifestly impossible and, here, undesirable. It is possible, however, to present very briefly a few official statements of policy which may prove to be landmarks in the development of Japanese and American reconstruction policy. A brief summary together with a word about the situations which occasioned them may assist in orienting the *Kokutai no Hongi.*

During the progress of the military phase of the War it was convenient and possibly justifiable to attack the enemy through all chinks in his armor. His philosophy, his Emperor, his religion, his education, his government, equally were the targets of the propaganda machines of the Allied Powers. But with defeat came a troubling responsibility. The United States, and presumably its allies, had to formulate a policy which would enable them to render impotent the forces within Japan which were officially considered responsible for the War, yet at the same time would not be an obvious repudiation of the basic philosophy which the victors outwardly professed. The United States established such a policy with its *Initial Post Surrender Policy for Japan,* prepared jointly by the Department of State, the War Department, and the Navy Department, and approved by the President of the United States on September 6, 1945. The ultimate objectives established by this policy were:

(a) To insure that Japan will not again become a menace to the United States or to the peace and security of the world.

(b) To bring about the eventual establishment of a peaceful and responsible government which will respect the rights of other states and will support the objectives of the United States as reflected in the ideals and principles of the Charter of the United Nations. The United States desires that the government should conform as closely as may be to principles of democratic self-government but it is not the responsibility of the Allied Powers to impose upon Japan any form of government not supported by the freely expressed will of the people.

The first of these two objectives was clearly punitive in intent. The maintenance of an Allied garrison force; the destruction of the Japanese military forces; the dissolution of the powerful Zaibatsu, or family industrial combines; the purge of dangerous and undesirable political officials; the restriction of industrial capacity, were obvious demilitarization procedures. But the second of these objectives was creative rather than destructive in nature. Here the sincere democratic nation was at a serious disadvantage.

It is possible to create dictatorial government by edict and compel compliance with force, but self-government by its very nature is something which must be wanted by the people who are to be governed. Experience has shown that this essential desire for political freedom is likely to develop only where certain conditions exist. Paramount among these is the condition of respect for the rights of the individual. Accordingly, one of the very earliest of the directives to the Imperial Japanese Government from the Supreme Commander for the Allied Powers was the so-called *Japanese Bill of Rights,* SCAP Directive of October 4, 1945. Paragraph *1a* of this directive assures freedom of thought, religion, assembly and speech. While establishing a situation favorable to the development of liberalism among the Japanese it also imposes definite restrictions on the actions and future policies of the Occupying Powers.

Retention of the Emperor as a puppet to assist in the peaceful control of the Japanese masses was an expedient which could perhaps be argued on the grounds of temporary military necessity but which was unpalatable to many on the grounds of compromise with the responsible leaders of the enemy. Yet an open attack on this traditional institution was not only probably futile but was also inconsistent with the avowed principles of freedom of religion. State Shinto had provided the fanatical driving force for the whole Japanese program of military expansion and ultranationalism. It still constituted a potential threat to a peaceful Asia. But if it were a religion, however repugnant, it had to be granted the same protection accorded other religions.

The school system had been used as a tool of unscrupulous propagandists. Its organization made it an appealing tool by which the Occupying Powers might in their turn exert an extremely efficient and powerful propaganda. But if the Japanese were not to exchange their own Japanese military dictatorship for an Occupation military dictatorship the educational system could not be cynically manipulated. Its teachers and students had to be given the opportunity to grow to the stature of self-government.

Radio, the press, the censorship of all communications offered efficient instruments for the control of Japanese thought. Such control would permit the Occupation authorities to use the masses to their ends with the same effectiveness that the Japanese military clique had previously used them to their ends. But again, such a policy would hardly be consistent with the promised freedom of thought and speech.

Actual policy was created in many ways. Basic statements were issued from time to time by the Department of State and the War Department in Washington. These usually established principles and goals rather than methods of accomplishing these goals. Almost always such statements were lacking in detail so that implementation policy had to be developed in Japan. Occasionally they were so general in wording that almost any interpretation was possible and directly contradictory policies were in fact enunciated to the Japanese, as in the control of scientific research, the degree of industrial dismemberment for reparations, and the importation of food for Japanese relief. The liaison between Japanese officials and Occupation officials created much of the working policy, popularly known as "government by nudge," never recorded but none-the-less effective. Informal contact between the personnel of the Occupying Powers and the Japanese people contributed to policy and frequently proved more effective than written statements. Policy was created by aroused public opinion, both in Japan and in the nations of the Occupying Powers. It was formed by the recognized but nonofficial recommendations of technical missions to Japan. It occasionally was formed through error—typographical, clerical, or translation—and by misinterpretation of the motives and actions of individuals holding official positions. One element should not be overlooked in appraising Occupation policy. Where minor deviations and inconsistencies have occurred they have come from misinterpreting the basic established policy. The goal was and is that of encouraging the Japanese to adopt voluntarily a form of self-government which is acceptable to the rest of the world, and not to impose a form of government which the people themselves reject.

The most important statement of policy concerning education was that of SCAP Directive AG 350 (22 October 45) CIE, "Administration of the Educational System of Japan." It attempted to define the broad areas of educational policy which were affected by the establishment of a Japanese Bill of Rights. It dealt with objectives of education, content of instruction, personnel of educational institutions, and the instrumentalities of educational processes such as textbooks, curricula, teaching manuals, radio, news, and schools. It directed a threefold control: scrutiny; punitive action against the undesirable; and encouragement of the desirable.

Obviously a formal statement of policy such as this had to be precise enough to establish definite goals and trends yet elastic enough to meet all contingencies. It could be effective only if supported with detailed instrumentation. This was accomplished informally by direct liaison with the Japanese officials concerned and formally through additional SCAP directives. Thus, the military arts (*budō*) were voluntarily suppressed by the Japanese officials themselves when they sensed from unofficial conferences that *budō* might otherwise become the target of much more severe official action. SCAP Directive AG 350 (30 October 45) CIE, "Investigation, Screening, and Certification of Teachers and Educational Officials," established a precedent by focusing Japanese attention on a necessary problem, the purge of militarists and ultranationalists from the schools, without detailing procedures by which the house-cleaning was to be accomplished. The necessity of producing an acceptable plan for a disagreeable task was considered an object lesson in democratic procedures and as such almost as important as the purge itself. SCAP Directive AG 000.8 (31 December 45) CIE, "Suspension of courses in Morals (*Shūshin*), Japanese History, and Geography," is perhaps the best example of the detailed directive in which the Japanese Imperial Government was told exactly how to put into effect some element of the general policy. It detailed procedures for eliminating objectionable Shinto teachings from curricula, textbooks, and teaching manuals and provided that courses in Geography, History, and Japanese Morals should be suspended until these deletions were accomplished and new materials were prepared.

The provisions of these several directives, together with the body of policy established by operational precedent in the Occupation, were canonized and lent official sanction by the Department of State statement, "Policy for the Revision of the Japanese Educational System," approved by the Far Eastern Commission (FEC) on March 27, 1947. The opening paragraph states:

Education should be looked upon as the pursuit of truth, as a preparation for life in a democratic nation, and as a training for the social and political responsibilities which freedom entails. Emphasis should be placed on the dignity and worth of the individual, on independent thought and initiative, and on developing a spirit of inquiry. The inter-dependent character of international life should be stressed. The spirit of justice, fair play, and respect for the rights of others, particularly minorities, and the necessity for friendship based upon mutual respect for people of all races and religions, should be emphasized. Special emphasis should also be placed on the teaching of the sanctity of the pledged word in all human relations, whether between individuals or nations. Measures should be taken as rapidly as possible to achieve equality of educational opportunity for all regardless of sex or social position. The revision of the Japanese educational system should in a large measure be undertaken by the Japanese themselves and steps should be taken to carry out such revision in accordance with the principles and objectives set forth in this paper.

The most important statement of policy concerning religion was that of SCAP Directive AG 000.3 (15 December 1945) CIE, "Abolition of Governmental Sponsorship, Support, Perpetuation, Control, and Dissemination of State Shinto." It is generally conceded to be the classic example of the type of implementing directive developed by sympathetic and detailed coöperation between the interested Japanese officials and the Occupation Authorities.

The problem was a delicate one. If the Emperor was to be permitted to continue as the temporal leader of the Japanese, how could he be stripped of his ecclesiastical position without an infringement upon his personal religious rights and those of his loyal followers? How could the masses of the Japanese people be delivered from the ideological bondage and financial burden of State Shinto without violating the personal religious liberties of the millions who apparently held this philosophy as a religious faith? Could an attack be made on a pernicious ideology without religious persecution?

United States policy on Shinto was first publicly enunciated in a radio broadcast by a Department of State official, John Carter Vincent, which was reported in Japan in the *Pacific Stars and Stripes,* newspaper of the United States military forces. A considerable Japanese reaction was anticipated and a request for a statement of official policy was referred to the Department of State. On October 13, 1945, the Secretary of State communicated the pertinent portion of the Vincent broadcast to the Headquarters of the Supreme Commander for the Allied Powers with the statement that it was a paraphrase of a State, War, and Navy Coördinating Committee (SWNCC) paper not yet received by Occupation Headquarters. The paraphrase stated:

Shintoism insofar as it is a religion of individual Japanese is not to be interfered with. Shintoism, however, insofar as it is directed by the Japanese Government and is a measure enforced from above by the Government, is to be done away with. People would not be taxed to support National Shinto and there will be no place for Shintoism in the schools. Shintoism as a State Religion, National Shinto, that is, will go. Our policy on this goes beyond Shinto. The dissemination of Japanese Militarists and ultra-Nationalistic ideology in any form will be completely suppressed and the Japanese Government will be required to cease financial and other support of Shinto establishments.

The leaders of the various religious bodies, including the officials of the Bureaus of Shrines and Religions and the heads of the thirteen Shinto Sects, voluntarily worked with the staff officers of the Occupation Headquarters in developing a practical and equitable implementation policy. This was issued by the Supreme Commander for the Allied Powers on December 15, 1945, and so perfectly had the preparatory staff work been done that not the slightest public resentment was discernible.

The final step in officially discarding the basic ideology which is expressed in the *Kokutai no Hongi* was accomplished on January 1, 1946, when Emperor Hirohito issued his *New Year's Rescript* in which he elected to retain his position as political leader of his people and to discard his dual role as religious leader. The official English translation of this document is reproduced in Appendix VI. There has never been a hint that this statement was anything but a perfectly free expression by the Emperor, completely uninspired by any suggestion or compulsion from Occupation Headquarters. It is probable that the editor and translator of *Kokutai no Hongi* were among the very few persons outside the Emperor's intimate Japanese advisors who knew the content of this Rescript before its release— when Mr. Gauntlett was asked by the Imperial Household to make the official translation. Obviously it was received with some degree of satisfaction by the Allies and has generally been considered one of the most important documents to come out of the War. But the Occidental observer would be naïve indeed if he did not recognize that this denial of the divinity of the Emperor and the racial superiority of the Japanese people falls far short of destroying the ideology expressed in the *Kokutai no Hongi.*

Were it ever expedient for a future Japanese government to resurrect the now discarded ideology it would not be necessary to claim coercion and a statement under duress. Continuity of the Imperial Line, even though in exile or reduced to the position of a puppet ruler, preserved in the past the essential element in the argument of divinity. Not even the wording of the opening articles of the new Constitution would seriously hamper such a possible future interpretation:

1. The Emperor shall be the symbol of the State and of the unity of the people, deriving his position from the will of the people with whom resides sovereign power.

2. The Imperial Throne shall be dynastic and succeeded to in accordance with the Imperial House Law passed by the Diet.

In November 1946 the Japanese Cabinet published a booklet entitled *Exposition on the New Constitution* in which the Government took the position that the *kokutai*, the national entity, had not undergone any change. An extended passage from this booklet is reproduced in Appendix VII. The *Kokutai no Hongi* is presented here as a historical document. May it not become a prophecy.

KOKUTAI NO HONGI

This book has been compiled in view of the pressing need of the hour to clarify our national entity and to cultivate and awaken national sentiment and consciousness.

Our national entity is vast and boundless, so that it is feared the book has fallen short in the penning of its true significance.

In quoting passages from the *Kojiki* and the *Nihon-shoki*, we have followed in the main the texts of the *Kokun Kojiki* and the *Nihon-shoki Tsūshaku*, and in the case of the names of the deities the *Nihon-shoki*.

Introduction

Our country faces a very bright future, blessed with a well-being that is indeed magnificent and with a very lively development abroad. Her industries are lively; her way of life has grown richer; and the progress made in the cultural fields merits attention. From of old, Oriental culture, which finds its origin in China and India, found its way into our country and was sublimated and fused into our "god-handed" national structure. And since the days of Meiji and Taishō, the various phases of our civilization have made remarkable strides through the introduction of modern European and American civilization. If one were to bring back to life today a Mannyō poet, whose culture was well-ordered, whose scholarship had made tremendous strides, and whose ideology and culture had reached the highest peak in richness, he would very likely sing again:

> How conscious am I of being alive—
> A loyal subject of my Lord!
> To think I live, when heaven and earth
> Are full of glory!

Through the great achievements of the Meiji Restoration, the people broke away from their old abuses, freed themselves of the feudal fetters, carried out their plans, and played their parts. Since then seventy years have passed, bringing with the lapse of time the realization of the great functions which we witness today.

Nevertheless, when we look back quietly on these great functions, there was by no means tranquillity or rest but immeasurable disquiet within and without, many difficulties in the path of advance, and much turmoil in the house of prosperity. In other words, the fundamental principles of our national entity tended to defy clarification. In the fields of scholastic pursuits, education, politics, economics, as well as in all fields of national life, there existed

many defects, and the cause behind the energy to grow and behind
the turmoil became intricate on the surface and below it. The
brilliant culture, too, came to have within it elements of richness
and of foulness. And thus are brought into being various and
knotty problems. At this time when our country is about to make
great strides, light and shadow seem to have appeared before us
hand in hand. However, this offers us nothing but a chance for
advancement and a time for progress; so that we must grasp the
real situation as it is at this time, in and outside the country, must
clarify the way we should take together, must stir ourselves to find
a way out of these difficult times, and must contribute all the more
toward the development of our national destiny.

The various ideological and social evils of present-day Japan
are the fruits of ignoring the fundamentals and of running into the
trivial, of lack in sound judgment, and of failure to digest things
thoroughly; and this is due to the fact that since the days of Meiji so
many aspects of European and American culture, systems, and
learning, have been imported, and that, too rapidly. As a matter
of fact, foreign ideologies imported into our country are in the main
the ideologies of enlightenment that have come down since the
eighteenth century, or their extensions. The views of the world
and of life that form the basis of these ideologies are a rationalism
and a positivism, lacking in historical views, which on the one
hand lay the highest value on, and assert the liberty and equality of,
individuals, and on the other hand lay value on a world by nature
abstract, transcending nations and races. Consequently, importance is laid upon human beings and their gatherings, who have
become isolated from historical entireties, abstract and independent of each other. It is political, social, moral, and pedagogical
theories based on such views of the world and of life, that have on
the one hand made contributions to the various reforms seen in
our country, and on the other have had deep and wide influence
on our nation's primary ideology and culture.

The movement for enlightenment in our country began with

the importation of the ideology of free rights of the people, which is the political philosophy of the period of enlightenment in France, and was followed by the introduction of such things as British and American conceptions of Parliamentary politics, materialism, utilitarianism, and German nationalism; and efforts were made to carry out reforms in our bigoted habits and institutions. Such a movement, under the name of civilization and enlightenment, was a marked trend of the times, and brought into being the so-called Age of Europeanization, by influencing politics, economics, concepts, and customs. There arose, however, a movement in the face of it for return to tradition. This was a movement carried out in the name of the preservation of national virtues, and was a manifestation of national consciousness against the tide of the surging importation of European culture. And indeed this was because there was danger of extreme Europeanization doing injury to our national tradition and corrupting the national spirit running through our history. This brought about a pitting of one against the other, of Europeanism and the principle of preservation of national traits, so that concepts became confused, the people being bewildered as to what to follow — national tradition, or new foreign ideas. But with the promulgation in 1890 of the Imperial Rescript on Education, the people came to discern the things accomplished by the Imperial Founder and Ancestors in the planting of virtues at the time of the founding of the nation, and herein they found a sure direction along which they should go. Nevertheless, in spite of the fact that this great Way based on this national entity was clearly manifested, foreign ideologies which remained as yet undigested led the fashion even in the days following, because importation of European civilization remained lively. In short, the concept of foreign individualism came in afresh and under a new ensign as positivism and as naturalism. Prior to and following this importation, idealistic concepts and scholastic theories were also brought in; and this was followed by the introduction of democracy, socialism, anarchism, communism, etc., and recent days saw the importation of Fascism; so that today we have reached a point where there has arisen an ideological and social confusion with which we are faced and wherein there has sprung up a fundamental awakening in regard to our national entity.

CONSCIOUSNESS OF OUR NATIONAL ENTITY

Paradoxical and extreme conceptions, such as socialism, anarchism, and communism, are all based in the final analyses on individualism which is the root of modern Occidental ideologies, and are no more than varied forms of their expressions. In the Occident, too, where individualism forms the basis of their ideas, they have, when it comes to communism, been unable to adopt it; so that now they are about to do away with their traditional individualism, which has led to the rise of totalitarianism and nationalism and incidentally to the upspringing of Fascism and Nazism. That is, it can be said that both in the Occident and in our country the deadlock of individualism has led alike to a season of ideological and social confusion and crisis. We shall leave aside for a while the question of finding a way out of the present deadlock, for, as far as it concerns our country, we must return to the standpoint peculiar to our country, clarify our immortal national entity, sweep aside everything in the way of adulation, bring into being our original condition,[1] and at the same time rid ourselves of bigotry, and strive all the more to take in and sublimate Occidental culture; for we should give to basic things their proper place, giving due weight to minor things, and should build up a sagacious and worthy[2] Japan. This means that the present conflict seen in our people's ideas, the

[1] A common Japanese phraseology which is based on the assumption that there is an "ideal" from which the people have or might have strayed, to which they should therefore return or at which they should aim.

[2] A coined idealistic epithet which defies translation, but which shows "bigness" in a comprehensive and spiritual sense, the characters forming the compound being something like "vast + quantity." The Japanese or *kun* pronunciation of the first of the characters is the same as that of another of the same meaning, but this character conveys a breadth wider and often spiritual.

unrest in their modes of life, the confused state of their civilization, can be put right only by a thorough investigation by us of the intrinsic nature of Occidental ideologies and by grasping the true meaning of our national entity. Then, too, this should be done not only for the sake of our nation but for the sake of the entire human race which is struggling to find a way out of the deadlock with which individualism is faced. Herein lies our grave cosmopolitan mission. It is for this reason that we have compiled the *Cardinal Principles of the National Entity of Japan,* to trace clearly the genesis of the nation's foundation, to define its great spirit, to set forth clearly at the same time the features the national entity has manifested in history, and to provide the present generation with an elucidation of the matter, and thus to awaken the people's consciousness and their efforts.

BOOK I
THE NATIONAL ENTITY OF JAPAN

I

The Founding of the Nation

The unbroken line of Emperors, receiving the Oracle of the Founder of the Nation, reign eternally over the Japanese Empire.[1] This is our eternal and immutable national entity. Thus, founded on this great principle, all the people, united as one great family nation in heart and obeying the Imperial Will, enhance indeed the beautiful virtues of loyalty and filial piety. This is the glory of our national entity. This national entity is the eternal and unchanging basis of our nation and shines resplendent throughout our history. Moreover, its solidarity is proportionate to the growth of the nation and is, together with heaven and earth, without end. We must, to begin with, know with what active brilliance this fountainhead shines within the reality of the founding of our nation.

BEGINNING OF HEAVEN AND EARTH[2]

Our nation was founded when its Founder, Amaterasu Ohmi-kami (Heavenly-Shining-Great-August-Deity), handed the Oracle to her Imperial Grandson Ninigi no Mikoto and descended to Mizuho no Kuni (Land of Fresh Rice-ears) at Toyoashihara (Rich Reed-plain). And in relating the facts of the founding of our Land by the Founder of our Empire, the *Kojiki* and the *Nihon-shoki* tell first of all of the beginning of heaven and earth, and of the making and consolidating, and the *Kojiki* says:

At the hour of the beginning of Heaven and Earth, the names of the deities that came into being in Takama no Hara (High-heaven-of plain)[3] were Ame no Minakanushi no Kami (Heaven-of-august-center-master-

---

[1]Or, more correctly: "The Japanese Empire [subj.], this [obj.] the Emperors of an eternal and single line, receiving [honorific] the Oracle of the Founder of the Nation, rule over eternally."

[2]The dawn of history; *anno mundi*.

[3]According to English syntax: Plain-of-High-Heaven.

of-deity),[4] next Takamimusubi no Kami (High-august-producing-of-deity), next Kamimusubi no Kami (Divine-producing-of-deity)[5]. These three deities were all deities that came into being singly, and hid their august persons.[6]

Again in the *Nihon-shoki,* it says:

Heaven was formed first and after that was Earth established. Thereafter were sacred deities brought forth betwixt them. Hence it is said that in the beginning of the dawn of the world the floating and drifting of the Land was, as it were, like unto the floating of a fish sporting on the face of the water. At that hour was a certain thing brought into being betwixt Heaven and Earth. Its shape was like unto a reed-shoot. Now, the deity into which it became transformed is called Kuni no Tokotachi no Mikoto (Land-of-eternal-stand-of-august-thing).[7]

Such folklore and legends have been our national beliefs since of old, and our nation springs from such a perpetual source.

THE MAKING AND CONSOLIDATING

And at the end of the days of the Seven Deities which began with Kuni no Tokotachi no Mikoto, the two deities, Izanagi no Mikoto (His Augustness the Male-who-invites) and Izanami no Mikoto (Her Augustness the Female-who-invites),[8] were born. According to the *Kojiki* these two Augustnesses, by complying with

---

[4]According to English syntax: Deity-(of)-August-center-master-of-Heaven. The English word "Deity" is used here and elsewhere for the Japanese word *Kami,* the conception of which is somewhat different from the Occidental idea of God.

[5]According to English syntax: Deity-(of)-High-august-producing, and Deity-(of)-Divine-producing. *Musubi* in these two names is interpreted by some authorities as meaning "wondrous producing" and by others as simply meaning "producing." See the section *"Musubi* and Harmony" in Book I, Chapter IV, for the official explanation of the original authors of the *Kokutai no Hongi.*

[6]See also B. H. Chamberlain, *op. cit.,* p. 15.

[7]See also W. G. Aston, *op. cit.,* Book I, pages 2-3.

[8]Aston, I, p. 6, footnote 4.

the divers decrees of the heavenly deities, completed the great task of making and consolidating the drifting Land. Namely, it is stated:

Hereupon the heavenly deities gave orders to the two deities, Izanagi no Mikoto (Male-who-invites-of-augustness) and Izanami no Mikoto (Female-who-invites-of-augustness)[9], decreeing that they "make, consolidate, and bring into being[10] this drifting land;" and granting unto them a heavenly jewelled spear, they entrusted them with the matter.[11]

AMATERASU OHMIKAMI (HEAVENLY-SHINING-GREAT-AUGUST-DEITY)

Thus, Izanagi no Mikoto and Izanami no Mikoto gave birth first to Oh-yashima (Great-Eight-Islands)[12] then gave birth to mountains and rivers, herbs and trees, and to deities, and furthermore gave birth to Amaterasu Ohmikami (Heavenly-Shining-Great-August-Deity),[13] who is the supreme deity who ruleth them, as stated in the *Kojiki:*

At this time Izanagi no Mikoto rejoiced exceedingly and said, "I have begotten and begotten children, and at the end of the begetting have ob-

---

[9]According to English syntax: His-Augustness-the-Male-who-invites, and, Her-Augustness-the-Female-who-invites. The existence of two schools of etymological explanations of the meaning of these names, basically different in their analyses but differing little in their meanings, is due to the fact that Chinese characters were used even in the oldest of Japanese books, the *Kojiki*, not only as ideographs having meaning, but also irrespective of their individual meanings to represent Japanese syllables, in the manner of *manyōgana* of a later date which were the forerunners of the present Japanese *kana*. One school divides *Izanagi* into *Iza* (come now!); *na* (thou); and *gi* (male). The other divides *Izanagi* into *Izana* (root of the verb *izanau,* invite); and *gi* (male).

[10]This idea of "making, consolidating, and bringing into being", always important in Japanese thought, was seized upon and applied by the Shintoists in relation to the Greater East Asia War (Dai Tōa Sensō). The explanation was made that Japan's mission in the war was reconstruction. The phrase was also used in connection with individual discipline.

[11]See also B. H. Chamberlain, *op. cit.,* p. 19.

[12]Another name for Japan.

[13]Commonly referred to as the Sun-Goddess.

tained three lofty children," and (overjoyed) swinging to and fro musically the necklace,[14] said the Amaterasu Ohmikami, "Reign thou over Takama no Hara (Plain-of-High-Heaven)," and so deigned to charge her.

Again, in the *Nihon-shoki* it says:

His Augustness Izanagi no Mikoto and Her Augustness Izanami no Mikoto consulted together and said: "We have already brought forth Oh-yashima no Kuni (Land-of-Great-Eight-Islands) as well as mountains, rivers, grasses and trees. Wherefore should we not bring forth one that shall be sovereign throughout the whole world?" They then together brought to birth the Sun Goddess. She is called Ohhirume no Muchi (Great-noon-female-of-possessor). In one place she is called Amaterasu Ohmikami. In another place she is called Amaterasu Ohhirume no Mikoto (Heaven-illumine-great-noon-female-of-augustness). The luster of this child was resplendent and shone throughout the six quarters.[15]

Amaterasu Ohmikami is called the Sun-Goddess or Ohhirume no Muchi (Great-noon-female-of-possessor), and as stated, "her resplendent luster shone throughout all the six quarters," and her august virtues are boundless and limitless, developing all things. In short, Amaterasu Ohmikami protects the deities of Takama no Hara (Plain of High Heaven) and the country begotten by the two Augustnesses, cherishes objects and causes them to grow and to prosper.

THE ORACLE AND THE DESCENT OF THE SUN-GODDESS'S GRANDSON

In order that this great Will and great task might flourish gloriously, coeternal with heaven and earth, Amaterasu Ohmikami caused her Grandson to descend, lay down the great principle touching the relationship between sovereign and subject, and firmly established the foundation of our nation's festivities, politics, and

[14]In ancient times both men and women decked themselves with chains of beads around their heads, necks, hands, legs, and clothes.

[15]East, West, South, North, Above, Below; hence, the world, the universe. See also Aston, I, page 18.

education. Herein was completed the great task of founding the country. Our country, having begun with the reality of such an eternal and profound beginning, grows and prospers together with heaven and earth without end, and manifests forth an "imposing ceremony," the like of which is indeed not seen among other nations.

Previous to the sending down by Amaterasu Ohmikami of her Imperial Grandchild Ninigi no Mikoto, the Deities of Izumo [Out-clouds] who clustered round Ohkuninushi no Kami [Deity-Master-of-Great-Land], the grandchild of her [i.e., Amaterasu Ohmikami's] younger brother Susano-o no Mikoto, observed the Imperial command with awe. Whereupon, it came about that the Imperial Grand-child should descend to Toyoashihara no Mizuho no Kuni [Land-of-fresh-rice-ears of Luxuriant-reed-plains].[16] Thus, it is stated in the Oracle which is coeval with heaven and earth and which was granted on the occasion of the descent to earth of the Imperial Grandchild:

Land-of-Fresh-ears-of-a-Thousand-Autumns — of [Long]-Five-Hun-dred-Autumns — of Luxuriant-Reed-Plains. This is the Land over which Our grandchildren are to reign. Go thou, Imperial Grandchild, and reign over it. Go thou free of trouble. As endless as Heaven and Earth shall the Imperial Throne prosper.[17]

It is in this manner that the great principle touching the relation-ship between sovereign and subject was made manifest and our national entity established. Thus it is, too, that the descendants of Amaterasu Ohmikami, the great reigning deity, descended to this Mizuho no Kuni, and that the prosperity of their Throne is together with heaven and earth without end. The great principle of the nation's beginning, therefore, is made manifest eternally and immutably on Toyoashihara no Mizuho no Kuni, through the advent of the Imperial Grandchild.

Again in the Oracle delivered on the occasion of the handing of the Divine Mirror, the Goddess says:

---

[16]One of the many flowery old names for Japan.
[17]From the *Nihon-shoki*. See also Aston, *op. cit.*, I, 77.

Honor this Mirror solely as Our soul, as ye would do Us reverence.[18] In effect, Amaterasu Ohmikami granted this Mirror as an (image) of her noble Spirit to her Grandchild, and the succeeding Emperors have handed it down (to their successors) and have reverenced it. The fact that they have handed down the Mirror means that they are always with Amaterasu Ohmikami: that is to say, Amaterasu Ohmikami is even now with the Mirror. The Emperors have constantly reverenced the Sacred Mirror, have had for their mind the mind of the great deity, and have been one in "essence" with the great deity. Herein lies the basis of our nation's piety and ancestor worship.

Again, she follows this Oracle, saying:

Let Omoikane no Kami [Thought-Includer-of-Deity] take charge of our affairs,[19] and govern.[20]

This Orace clearly shows that Omoikane no Kami should constantly take in hand the affairs before [her august Spirit] and govern; and it solemnly sets forth the relationship between the Emperors, who are deities incarnate,[21] being grandchildren of the great deity, and those who govern through the Emperors' commands. The government of our country is administered by the Emperor, who on the one hand worships the spirits of his Imperial Ancestors and on the other as deity incarnate leads his people; and those who govern, receiving the great august mind, [must] manifest their utmost sincerity as counselors. Hence, the government of our country is a sacred undertaking and by no means a private affair.

In order, therefore, to clarify the essential qualities of the Emperor and to clarify still further our national entity, one must make

---

[18]From the *Kojiki*. See also Chamberlain, *op. cit.,* p. 130.

[19]*Mimae no koto,* lit. "august-fore-of-things", or roughly, "affairs before (Her) august spirit." The spirit of *Amaterasu Ohmikami* is considered to have concern for and to direct everything in the realm, and hence, to guide the affairs of state.

[20]See also Chamberlain, *op. cit.,* p. 130.

[21]Literally, Present-August-Deities.

clear the significance of [the Throne's being] coeval with heaven and earth, the unbroken line of Emperors, and of the Three Sacred Treasures of the Imperial Court.

THE THRONE'S BEING COEVAL WITH HEAVEN AND EARTH

By being coeval with heaven and earth is meant to be endless together with heaven and earth. It seems that one has not yet quite fathomed the full import of endlessness if one thinks of it as being successions of time. Ordinarily, words such as "eternity" or "endlessness" convey simply the ideas of perpetuity in successions of time; but the so-called expression, "coeval with heaven and earth," has a far deeper significance. That is to say, it expresses eternity and at the same time signifies the present. In the great august Will and great august undertakings of the Emperor, who is deity incarnate, is seen the great august Will of the Imperial Ancestors, and in this Will lives the endless future of our nation. That our Imperial Throne is coeval with heaven and earth means indeed that the past and the future are united in one in the "now," that our nation possesses everlasting life, and that it flourishes endlessly. Our history is an evolution of the eternal "now," and at the root of our history there always runs a stream of eternal "now."

In the Imperial Rescript on Education, the Emperor [Meiji] says:

Guard and maintain the prosperity of Our Imperial Throne coeval with heaven and earth.

And this is brought to fruition where the subjects render service to the Emperor—who takes over and clarifies the teachings bequeathed by the Imperial Ancestors—accept the august Will, and walk worthily in the Way. Thus, sovereign and subject, united in one, take shape and develop eternally, and the Imperial Throne goes on prospering. Truly, the Imperial Throne, which is coeval with heaven and earth, forms the basis of our national entity; and that which in the beginning of the founding of the nation firmly established this, is the Oracle coeval with heaven and earth.

THE LINE OF EMPERORS UNBROKEN FOR AGES ETERNAL

The Imperial Throne is the Throne of a line of Emperors un-broken for ages eternal, and is the Emperors' Throne[22] of a truly single line. The Imperial Throne is the Throne of the Sovereign Lords who are the deific offspring of the Imperial Ancestor, who inherit the Land founded by the Imperial Ancestors, and make it their great august task to govern it peacefully as a peaceful Land,[23] and is the station of the Emperors who, one with the Imperial Ancestor, manifest their great august Will even until now, and who cause the Land to prosper and care for the people. The subjects, in looking up to the Emperor, who is deity incarnate, reverence at the same time the Imperial Ancestors, and under his bounty become the subjects of our country. Thus, the Imperial Throne is a Throne of the utmost dignity and is the foundation of a Land eternally firm.

That the Emperor who accedes to the Throne is descended from an unbroken line of sovereigns is the basis of the founding of the Land, and is that which the Oracle clearly sets forth. Namely, that the offspring of Amaterasu Ohmikami accede to the Throne from generation to generation is a great law which is forever unalterable. It indeed seems inevitable that in foreign countries where conglom-erations of individuals form a nation, rulers, on a basis of intelli-gence, virtues, and power, accede to a position because of their vir-tues, those without virtues leaving their positions, or that they rise to positions of governors through power, and [it seems inevitable, too] that they are, through loss of power, deprived of their position, or also that they, completely subject to the people who exercise power, are chosen by election, etc., and that decisions regarding them are purely the result of men's doings and men's influences. More-over, as for these virtues and power, they are correlative, so that of necessity conflicts arise through the influence of power and per-

---

[22]Here the phraseology for the "Emperors' Throne" is *Amatsuhitsugi* (Succession of Heaven's Sun).

[23]*Yasu-kuni.* Cf. Yasukuni Shrine (Peaceful Land Shrine), in which the spirits of those who have died fighting for the country are enshrined.

sonal interests, and this naturally makes a nation subject to revolutions. In our country, however, the Imperial Throne is acceded to by one descended from a line of Emperors unbroken for ages eternal, and is absolutely firm. Consequently, the Emperor, who sits upon such an Imperial Throne, is naturally endowed with gracious virtues, so that the Throne is so much the firmer and is also sacred. That the subjects should serve the Emperor is not because of duty as such, nor is it submission to authority; but is the welling, natural manifestation of the heart and is the spontaneous obedience of deep faith toward His Majesty. We subjects hold in awe the cause behind the "growing" prosperity of the Imperial Line and its dignity, of which there is no parallel in foreign countries.

THE THREE SACRED TREASURES

Symbolic of the Imperial Throne are the Three Sacred Treasures [of the Imperial Court]. In the *Nihon-shoki* it is stated:

Amaterasu Ohmikami, therefore, gave unto Amatsuhikohikoho no Ninigi no Mikoto the Three Treasures, namely, the curved jewel of Yasaka gem, the eight-hand Mirror, and the Sword Kusanagi.[24]
These Three Sacred Treasures of the Imperial Court are of three kinds: the Curved Jewels of Yasakani and the Mirror of Yata, presented in front of the cavern of Heaven, and the Sword of Ame no Murakumo [i.e., the Sword of Kusanagi] granted by Susano-o no Mikoto. The Imperial Ancestor particularly granted these Treasures on the occasion of the Imperial Grandchild's descent to earth; and ever since, the Sacred Treasures have become the august symbol of the Throne who from generation to generation uninterruptedly hands them down. Consequently, the successive generations of Emperors, upon the occasion of succession to the Imperial Throne, receive them, and transmit the great august Will of Amaterasu Ohmikami in full, and in particular consecrate the Sacred Mirror as [an image] of the Imperial Ancestor's noble Spirit.

---

[24]See also Aston, *op. cit.,* I, 76.

His Majesty the Present Emperor graciously says in the Imperial rescript of his august enthronement:

We, through the resplendent Spirit of Our Ancestors, reverently succeed to the Imperial Line, with awe receive the Sacred Treasures, and herein do perform the rite of enthronement and declare [the same] to you subjects.

Thus, as regards the Three Sacred Treasures of the Imperial Court, there are those who take them as setting forth the cardinal points of government, while there are others who look upon them as setting forth the principles of morality. And these views should be regarded as flowing out spontaneously from the hearts of the people who reverence all the more the sanctity of the Sacred Treasures.

II

The Sacred Virtues

THE EMPEROR

The making and consolidating by the two Augustnesses, Izanagi no Mikoto and Izanami no Mikoto, saw the founding of the Land through the Oracle of Amaterasu Ohmikami who received their great august Will. Later, there followed the inauguration of the Emperor Jimmu [B.C. 660], and then the great august tasks of the successive Emperors, the nation thus continuing to prosper. Through the two Augustnesses, Oh-yashima was brought to birth, and through the Oracle of Amaterasu Ohmikami, the nation began. Of the august virtues of Amaterasu Ohmikami the *Nihon-shoki* says: "The resplendent luster shone throughout all the six quarters." The Emperor embodies the august virtues of the Imperial Ancestor who shines throughout all the six quarters, takes over the august injunctions of the Imperial Ancestors, and reigns endlessly over our country. Consequently, the subjects, receiving as their own the Emperor's great august Will, deign to assist in the "god-handed" activities. Herein is the Empire's establishment and its endless prosperity.

The Emperor is an august descendant of Amaterasu Ohmikami, Taika in the decree following the carrying out of the new administration:[1]

As deity [We] deigned to charge Our child to rule.[2] Therefore, since the beginning of Heaven and Earth, this country is a Land which the sovereigns[3] rule.

---

[1]Reform of the Taika Era [A.D. 645-649]. It should be noted that although 649 is considered the end of the era it does not mark the end of the Reform.

[2]This is a repetition of what Amaterasu Ohmikami said when she charged her grandchild Ninigi no Mikoto to rule the country.

[3]The sovereigns who are the descendants.

Again, His Majesty the Present Emperor says in the Rescript issued on the occasion of the enthronement ceremony:

Know ye, Our subjects,[4] Our Imperial Ancestors, following the great Way of the deities, have conducted the heavenly duties,[5] have established the foundation everlastingly[6] unchangeable, have transmitted the endless Throne of a single infinite lineage, and thus [this] has come to reach Our Person.

Hereby we behold the great august Will of the Emperors, who succeed to an Imperial Throne unbroken for ages eternal, to follow the great Way of the deities and all the more to conduct the heavenly duties.

That the Emperor Jimmu said, "Whither shall We go that We may rule the realm in peace?" when he conferred with his Imperial elder brother, Itsuse no Mikoto, at the Palace of Takachiho, was a manifestation of his great august Will to take special thought over the country and to love his subjects. And this is also the august spirit of the successive Emperors. On the occasion of the enthronement the Emperor Jimmu did say in his proclamation:

It is six years since We repaired to the East. Through the influence of the heavenly deities[7] the enemies have been subdued. Though the out-of-the-way lands are not yet pacified and the unsubdued remnants are wild, the central lands[8] are free of turmoil. Do ye your best to enlarge the Imperial capital and build ye the Palace. Would it not be good, too, thereafter to unify the six quarters, to establish the capital, and to make [one] house by covering the eight corners?[9]

This proclamation did disperse evil, lay down the Way, and set forth our country's resplendent way of progress which increasingly grows wider. Thus this is verily the great policy of the successive Emperors who without a break succeed each other.

---

[4]Literally, "We deem that . . ."
[5]The tasks of the Emperors.
[6]Literally, ten thousand generations.
[7]The deities at Takama no Hara, including Amaterasu Ohmikami.
[8]The Yamato region.
[9]The ends of the earth.

Hence, the Emperor is a deity incarnate who rules our country
in unison with the august Will of the Imperial Ancestors. We do
not mean, when respectfully referring to him as deity incarnate—
marvelous[10] deity—or humanly manifested deity, the so-called absolute God or omniscient and omnipotent God, but signify that the
Imperial Ancestors have manifested themselves in the person of the
Emperor, who is their divine offspring, that the Emperor in turn
is one in essence[11] with the Imperial Ancestors, that he is forever
the fountainhead for the growth and development of his subjects
and the country, and that he is endlessly a superbly august person.
Article I of the Imperial Constitution which has it that

The Empire of Japan shall be reigned over and governed by a line
of Emperors unbroken for ages eternal,[12]

and also Article III which has it that "The Emperor is sacred and
inviolate," are things that clarify the august nature of the Emperor.
Wherefore, the Emperor differs from the sovereigns of foreign
countries, is not a ruler set up by reason of necessity for the administration of a country, nor is he a sovereign chosen and settled upon
by the subjects on grounds of intelligence or virtues.

PIETY

The Emperor is an august descendant of Amaterasu Ohmikami,
and is a divine offspring of the Imperial Ancestors. The Emperor's
Throne is stately and weighty, and this is because he accedes to the
Throne as a descendant of the deities in heaven. In the proclamation
issued on the occasion of the Emperor Mommu's enthronement
[A.D. 697] His Majesty did say:

Just as charged by the deities who sit in Heaven, though an august
child of the deities in Heaven, in the sequence in which the Princes of

---

[10]Also "efficacious."

[11]Literally, "august one body."

[12]Accepted translation, but literally, "The Empire of Japan, this a line of
Emperors unbroken for ages eternal shall reign over and govern." This refers, of course, to the "old" or 1889 Constitution.

the Blood are born, according to the order in which one is made to govern this Land of Oh-yashima since the generations of the distant Ancestors of the Emperors began to administer in Takama no Hara even
until now.[13]

Just so, the successive Emperors have revered the Imperial Ancestors as the descendants of the deities of heaven and, being one in
essence with the Imperial Ancestors, do sit upon the Throne. Consequently, beginning with the Emperor Jimmu, who of old established a place of divine service on Mount Tomi and who, deifying
the Imperial ancestral deities in heaven, expounded the great way
of filial piety, the successive Emperors one and all venerate the
divine spirits of the Imperial Ancestors, and personally conduct
the religious rites.

The Emperor most solemnly conducts the religious rites both
regular and extraordinary. These rites mean that the Emperor, ven-
erating in person the divine spirits of the Imperial Ancestors, increasingly becomes one in essence with the Imperial Ancestors, and
by this means he prays for the well-being of the people and the
prosperity of the nation. Again, he has since of old laid importance
on festivals having to do with agriculture, and in the great harvest
festival which comes but once during one reign and in the annual
harvest festival, he spends a whole night in conducting the festival
in person. This practice originates from the fact that, on the occasion
of the descent of the Imperial Grandchild, Amaterasu Ohmikami
simultaneously with the granting of the Oracle and the Sacred
Treasures did bestow the ears of rice at the place of divine service.
In the Oracle delivered on the occasion, she says:

With the ears of rice at the place of divine service eaten in *Takama no
Hara* We also feed Our child.

Therefore, in the great harvest festival and the [annual] harvest
festival is clearly witnessed the august spirit of the divine ages in the

---

[13]The passage seems to leave much to one's imagination, being "unfinished."

revering of the ears of rice handed in person by the Imperial Ancestor and in the tender care for the people of the Land of Mizuho [Fresh rice ears].

CONCORD OF RELIGIOUS RITES, ADMINISTRATION, AND EDUCATION

The Emperors become one in essence with the Imperial Ancestors through the religious rites and, responding to the august spirit of the Imperial Ancestors, rear their people and cause them to prosper, a people over whom they have reigned. Here is witnessed the august spirit of the Emperors who rule the country. Therefore, the conducting of the religious rites and the work of administration are in their principle united. Also, the Emperors hand over the august injunctions of the Imperial Ancestors, and thereby make clear the great principle of the founding of the nation and the great Way which the people should follow. Here lies the basic principle of our education. Wherefore, education too is in its essence united with the religious rites and government. In short, religious rites, government, and education, each fulfilling its function, are entirely one.

THE AUGUST SPIRIT OF NATIONAL ADMINISTRATION

The great august Will of the Emperor in the administration of the nation is constantly clearly reflected in our history. This Land was made and consolidated by Izanagi no Mikoto and Izanami no Mikoto in compliance with the divers orders given by the heavenly deities. And Ninigi no Mikoto, receiving the Oracle of Amaterasu Ohmikami and descending to earth at the head of many deities, set the eternally unchangeable foundation of our nation. After that, every generation up to His Augustness Hikonagisatake-ugayafukia-ezu no Mikoto[14] was intent in his desire for the cultivation of righteousness; and on reaching the generation of the Emperor Jim-

---

[14] A son of Hiko-hohodemi no Mikoto and Toyotama Hime. He married Tamayori Hime, a younger sister of his mother, and had four sons of whom the last was the Emperor Jimmu.

mu, the capital was established in Yamato, and the subjects were governed. And replying on the one hand to the august benevolence seen in the granting of the Land by the Imperial Ancestor to the Grandchild,[15] he spread abroad, on the other hand, the august Will to cultivate righteousness as fostered by the Imperial Grandchild. Hence, the august spirit in which the Land has been administered by the successive Emperors, based solely on the great august Will seen in the sending down to earth of the Imperial Grandchild by the Imperial Ancestor, is seen in their keeping the Land at peace, and in making the influence of the august benevolence in educating, enlightening, and guiding the people, felt everywhere. During the reign of the Emperor Sujin [B.C. 97-30], on the occasion of the dispatch of the four war lords to the four districts,[16] too, this august spirit is clearly seen. Namely, in the proclamation the Emperor says:

The key to leading the people doth lie in teaching and transforming them. Now already the deities of heaven and earth have been reverenced, so that all ill and harm have died out throughout the Land. Howbeit, barbarians in far-off places have not yet received the law; and is it not because these have not even till now known the Sovereign's teachings? Hence, choose ye courtiers, dispatch them everywhere, and cause them to know Our laws.

The case is identical when, in the reign of the Emperor Keikō [A.D. 71-130], His Majesty caused His Augustness Yamatotakeru no Mikoto [A.D. 81-113][17] to subdue the Kumaso and the Ezo.[18] Again, the dispatching of an expedition to Shiragi[19] [A.D. 201-269] by the Empress Jingō, the causing of Sakanoue no Tamuramaro

---

[15]Literally, "heaven-spirit-grant-land."

[16]The seven words are a translation of *Shidō-Shōgun, Shidō* meaning "four *dō*," i.e., Hokurikudō, Tōkaidō, San-in-dō, and San-yō-dō, which cover nearly the whole of Honshū, to which four members of the Imperial Family were sent to disseminate culture.

[17]The most famous hero of legendary times.

[18]The Kumaso were ancient inhabitants of Kyūshū whose subjection took several centuries, while the Ezo (Yezo) are reported to have come from abroad.

[19]Silla, one of the ancient kingdoms of Korea (B.C. 57-A.D. 934).

[A.D. 758-811] by the Emperor Kammu [A.D. 781-805] to subdue the Land of Oh-u[20] and in recent times the Sino-Japanese and Russo-Japanese Wars, the annexation of Korea, and the efforts exerted in the founding of Manchoukuo, are one and all but expressions of the great august Will replying to the august benevolence seen in the granting of the Land by the Imperial Ancestor to the Grandchild,[21] on the one hand, and on the other the promoting of the peace of the country and the advancement of the great task of love for the people, thus radiating the grace of the Imperial Throne. The Emperor Meiji sang:

> Should we not preserve in dignity
> > This Land of Peace[22]
> > > Handed down from the age of the gods?

> Following the ancient days of sages,
> > Would We rule Our Land of Reed-plains.[23]

Thus do we witness [in these two poems] the great august Will of the Emperor.

LOVE FOR THE PEOPLE

Evidences of the Emperor's endless love and care for his subjects are constantly seen throughout history. The Emperor graciously treats his subjes as *ohmitakara,*[24] loves and protects them as one

---

[20]The former provinces of Mutsu and Dewa, comprising the whole northern part of the island of Honshū.

[21]Literally, "heaven-spirit-grant-land."

[22]Urayasu no Kuni, another name for Japan.

[23]This poem was composed in 1904, while the preceding poem was composed later, in 1910.

[24]One of a multitude of names for "subjects" or "people," whose denotation is "great treasures," but which has practically lost this sense.

would sucklings, and, depending upon their coöperation, diffuses his policies widely. With this great august Will the successive Emperors directed their august minds towards the happiness of their subjects, not merely encouraging them to do what is right but pitying and putting aright those who had gone astray.

Again, when Amaterasu Ohmikami advised the deities of Izumo to swear allegiance prior to sending down the Imperial Grandchild to earth, she had peaceful measures for her principles; and on the swearing of allegiance by Ohkuninushi no Mikoto, she builded a palace and treated him with respect. This is why even unto this day the Grand Shrine of Izumo is held in high regard. Benevolence such as this is [seen in] the august Will of the Emperors who, since the days of the Imperial Ancestor, constantly reign over this Land.

There is no need to take the trouble to explain how the successive Emperors counted it their duty to nurture their subjects, to provide them with ample clothing and food, to remove their disasters, and intently to set their minds at rest. The Emperor Suinin [B.C. 29-A.D. 70] had many ponds and ditches built, encouraged farming, and thereby enriched the people's[25] means of livelihood. Again, the august sympathy shown by the Emperor Nintoku [A.D. 313-399], who exercised solicitude for the well-being of the people, is a subject widely related and lauded by the people. The Emperor Yūryaku [A.D. 457-479] says in his posthumous proclamation:

Both Our body and mind are together become sick. Such a thing as this is from the beginning not on account of Ourselves alone; but [because] We wish to have Our subjects live in peace.

Then again, such historic facts as the following move us subjects to tears: namely, how on a cold night the Emperor Daigo [A.D. 898-930] took off his robes to think over the conditions of his subjects—how the Emperor Go-Daigo [A.D. 1319-1338], hearing of

---

[25]*Ohmitakara.* See previous note. While *hiragana* is used in the preceding example, characters are used here, which are those for the modern *hyakushō*, farmer, which formerly stood for "people," the characters being a combination of "hundred" and "surnames."

the famine throughout the country, said, "If there is anything for which We are to blame, may Heaven punish Us alone. Through what fault are the subjects meeting with this calamity?"—and how he went without his breakfast in order to give to the famished and those stricken with poverty—and also how many deaths among the people brought about by an epidemic caused the Emperor Go-Nara [A.D. 1527-1557] a great deal of solicitude.

The Emperor does not look upon his subjects as just his own, but as descendants of the subjects of the Imperial Ancestors. In the Imperial Rescript issued on the occasion of the promulgation of the Constitution, the Emperor Meiji says: "We recall the fact that Our subjects are descendants of the Imperial Ancestors' good and faithful subjects."

Again, the Emperor Meiji says in his Imperial letter at the time of the Reformation in the first year of Meiji:

On this occasion when the administration of the whole country is undergoing a complete change, should there be even one person among the entire nation that is unable to pass his days in peace, We are to blame; so that We Ourselves will exert every ounce of effort and with all Our heart and will take the lead in the matter of hardships, follow the path taken by Our Ancestors, and make Our Administration bear fruit. Thus only shall We fulfil Our inherited divine mission and be worthy of being the Ruler of Our subjects.

And when we read in one of the Emperor's poems:

> O that Our subjects were sound in health
> Who each in his own sphere toils!

we respectfully witness the Emperor's august compassion which exceeds a parent's love for his child. The Emperor's deeds that remain with us are so many as to defy enumeration when we cite such things as how he enshrines as deities in Yasukuni Shrine those loyal subjects that have sacrificed their lives for the nation since about the time of the Restoration, lauding their meritorious deeds without regard to standing or position, and how he poured out his great august heart in giving relief in times of natural calamities. Furthermore, with a deep august benevolence that pities sin[26] he forgives even those subjects who have committed misdeeds.

Also, the successive Emperors have taken pains to show us the Way which the subjects should observe. Namely, the reign of the Empress Suiko [A.D. 593-628] saw the establishment of a Code of Laws in Seventeen Chapters[27] and in recent times in the twenty-third year of Meiji, the Emperor Meiji granted the Imperial Rescript on Education. So endlessly great are the Imperial virtues, who is there that cannot but be deeply impressed!

---

[26]*Tsumi*, translated "sin," is practically confined to breaches of the law, since "sin" in the Christian sense is little understood.

[27]*Kempō Jūshichijō*, whose publication is ascribed by the *Nihon-shoki* (also known as the *Nihongi*) to (Prince) Shōtoku Taishi. It is a compilation of moral precepts, borrowed from Buddhism, Confucianism, and Shinto.

III

The Way of the Subjects

THE SUBJECTS

We have already witnessed the boundless Imperial virtues. Wherever this Imperial virtue of compassion radiates, the Way for the subjects naturally becomes clear. The Way of the subjects exists where the entire nation serves the Emperor united in mind in the very spirit in which many deities served at the time when the Imperial Grandchild, Ninigi no Mikoto, descended to earth. That is, we by nature[1] serve the Emperor and walk the Way of the Empire, and it is perfectly natural that we subjects should possess this essential quality.

We subjects are intrinsically quite different from the so-called citizens of Occidental countries. The relationship between ruler and subject is not of a kind in which the people are correlated to the sovereign or in which there is first a people for whose prosperity and well-being a ruler is established. But the reason for erring as to the essential qualities of these subjects or for looking upon them as being the same as so-called citizens, or again for failure to show that at least there is a distinct difference between the two, [all of] which happens oftentimes, is that a clear-cut view concerning the cardinal principles of our national entity is lacking and confusion arises as a result of an ambiguous understanding of foreign theories about States. When citizens who are conglomerations of separate individuals independent of each other give support to a ruler in correlation to the ruler, there exists no deep foundation between ruler and citizen to unite them. However, the relationship between the Emperor and his subjects arises from the same fountainhead, and has prospered ever since the founding of the nation as one in essence. This is our nation's great Way and consequently forms the

---

[1] In the way we are born, from the time we are born, etc., would be nearer to the Japanese.

source of the Way of our subjects, and there is a radical difference between [ours] and foreign countries in the matter of choice. Needless to say, even in foreign countries their respective histories, as betwen ruler and citizens, differ, and there are bonds that attend these relationships. Nevertheless, a country such as ours which, since its founding, has seen a Way "naturally" one in essence with nature and man united as one, and which thereby has prospered all the more, cannot find its counterpart among foreign countries. Herein lies our national entity which is unparalleled in the world, and the Way of our subjects has its reason for being simply on the basis of this national entity, and on this, too, are based loyalty and filial piety.

LOYALTY AND PATRIOTISM

Our country is established with the Emperor, who is a descendant of Amaterasu Ohmikami, as her center, and our ancestors as well as we ourselves constantly behold in the Emperor the fountainhead of her life and activities. For this reason, to serve the Emperor and to receive the Emperor's great august Will as one's own is the rationale of making our historical "life" live in the present; and on this is based the morality of the people.

Loyalty means to reverence the Emperor as [our] pivot and to follow him implicitly. By implicit obedience is meant casting ourselves aside and serving the Emperor intently. To walk this Way of loyalty is the sole Way in which we subjects may "live," and the fountainhead of all energy. Hence, offering our lives for the sake of the Emperor does not mean so-called self-sacrifice, but the casting aside of our little selves to live under his august grace and the enhancing of the genuine life of the people of a State. The relationship between the Emperor and the subjects is not an artificial relationship [which means] bowing down to authority, nor a relationship such as [exists] between master and servant as is seen in feudal morals. That means to take a stand at the "source" through the "parts," and to manifest the "source" by fulfilling the "parts." The ideology which interprets the relationship between the Emperor and his subjects as being a reciprocal relationship such as merely [involves] obedience to authority or rights and duties, rests on individualistic ideologies, and is a rationalistic way of thinking that looks on everything as being in equal personal relationships. An individual is an existence belonging to a State and her history which form the basis of his origin, and is fundamentally one body with it. However, even if one were to think of a nation contrariwise and also to set up a morality by separating the individual alone from this one body, with this separated individual as the basis, one would only end in a so-called abstract argument that has lost its basis.

In our country, the two Augustnesses, Izanagi no Mikoto and Izanami no Mikoto, are ancestral deities of nature and the deities, and the Emperor is the divine offspring of the Imperial Ancestor who was born of the two Augustnesses. The Imperial Ancestor and the Emperor are in the relationship of parent and child, and the relationship between the Emperor and his subjects is, in its righteousness, that of sovereign and subject and, in its sympathies, that of father and child. This relationship is an "essential"[2] relationship that is far more fundamental than the rational, obligatory relationships, and herein are the grounds that give birth to the Way of loyalty. From the point of individualistic personal relationships, the relationship between sovereign and subject in our country may [perhaps] be looked upon as that between non-personalities. However, this is nothing but an error arising from treating the individual as supreme, from the notion that has individual thoughts for its nucleus, and from personal abstract consciousness. Our relationship between sovereign and subject is by no means a shallow, lateral relationship such as [means] the correlation between ruler and citizen, but is a relationship springing from a basis transcending

---

[2] In the sense of having to do with natural qualities.

this correlation, and is that of self-effacement and a return to [the] "one,"[3] in which this basis is not lost. This is a thing that can never be understood from an individualistic way of thinking. In our country, this great Way has seen a natural development since the founding of the nation, and the most basic thing that has manifested itself as regards the subjects is in short this Way of loyalty. Herein exists the profound meaning and lofty value of loyalty. Of late years, through the influence of the Occidental individualistic ideology, a way of thinking which has for its basis the individual has become lively. Consequently, this and the true aim[4] of our Way of loyalty which is "essentially" different from it are not necessarily [mutually] consistent. That is, those in our country who at the present time expound loyalty and patriotism are apt to lose [sight of] its true significance, being influenced by Occidental individualism and rationalism. We must sweep aside the corruption of the spirit and the clouding of knowledge that arises from setting up one's "self" and from being taken up with one's "self" and return to a pure and clear state of mind that belongs intrinsically to us as subjects, and thereby fathom the great principle of loyalty.

The Emperor always honors[5] the Imperial Ancestors, and, taking the lead of his subjects, shows by practice the oneness of ancestor and offspring, and sets an example of reverence for the deities and for the ancestors. Again, we subjects, as descendants of subjects who served the Imperial Ancestors, revere their ancestors, inherit their motives of loyalty, make this [spirit] "live" in the present, and pass it on to posterity. Thus, reverence for the deities and for the ancestors and the Way of loyalty are basically entirely one, and are Ways essentially inseparable. Such unity is seen in our country alone, and here, too, is the reason why our national entity is sacred.[6]

---

[3] "Self-effacement and return to [the] one" is represented by four characters: "sink-self-return-one," and may be paraphrased as, "casting oneself away and returning to the one great Way."

[4] Or, spirit.

[5] Or, worships. The word is connected with Shintoism and can be variously rendered.   [6] Or, august.

The perfect unity between reverence for the deities and the Way of loyalty is also accounted for by the fact that these things and patriotism are one. To begin with, our country is one great family nation [comprising] a union[7] of sovereign and subject, having the Imperial Household as the head family, and looking up to the Emperor as the focal point from of old to the present. Accordingly, to contribute to the prosperity of the nation is to serve for the prosperity of the Emperor; and to be loyal to the Emperor means nothing short of loving the country and striving for the welfare of the nation. Without loyalty there is no patriotism, and without patriotism there is no loyalty. All patriotism is always impregnated with the highest sentiments of loyalty, and all loyalty is always attended with the zeal of patriotism. Of course, in foreign countries, too, there exists a spirit of patriotism. But this patriotism is not of a kind which, like in our country, is from the very roots one with loyalty and in perfect accord[8] with reverence for the deities and the ancestors.

Indeed, loyalty is our fundamental Way as subjects, and is the basis of our national morality. Through loyalty are we become Japanese subjects; in loyalty do we obtain life; and herein do we find the source of all morality. According to our history, the spirit of loyalty always runs through the hearts of the people. The decline of the Imperial Court in the Age of Civil Wars[9] deeply moves one to awe;[10] but in this age, too, a hero in carrying out some undertaking could not win the hearts of the people so long as a spirit of reverence for the Emperor was not given recognition. The ability of Oda Nobunaga [A.D. 1534-1582] and Toyotomi Hideyoshi [A.D. 1536-1598] to reap the fruits of their enterprises speaks for the state

---

[7]Literally, "one body."

[8]Or, agreement; unity.

[9]Sengoku Jidai, from 1490 to 1600, during which Japan was completely involved in civil war.

[10]The predicate is a common Japanese expression used with regard to the Imperial Household which carries with it a sense of the deepest awe, and for which there is no adequate translation.

of affairs at the time. That means that under all circumstances the spirit of reverence for the Emperor is the most powerful thing that moves the nation.

We read in a poem by Ohtomo no Yakamochi [died A.D. 785] in the *Mannyōshū*:

> One known as Ohkumenushi,
> A far-off ancestor of Ohtomo,
> That rendered the Emperor service
> Vowed, "If I traversed the sea,
> A watery corse I'd be;
> If mountains I traversed,
> A grassy corse I'd lie;
> If I could only die
> Beside my Emperor,
> Let come what will!"

This song has touched our people's heartstrings since of old, and is still handed down to and sung by us.

In a poem by Tachibana no Moroe [A.D. 684-757][11] which reads:

> Were I to serve my Lord until
> My hair turned white as the falling snow,
> How exalted I should feel!

a loyalty in serving the Emperor until one's hair turned white is vividly manifested. Then again, Kusunoki Masashige's [A.D. 1294-1336][12] spirit to serve the nation over seven spans of life[13] is even now stirring the people to the depths. Also, in our country, since of old, there have been not a few utterances in the way of poems expressive of the spirit of loyalty [composed] at white heat or in deep pain. For instance, such are:

---

[11]One of the compilers of the *Mannyōshū*. Ohtomo no Yakamochi is believed also to have been a compiler.

[12]A member of renowned family of *daimyō* (feudal lords); descended from Tachibana no Moroe.

[13]Literally, "seven-lives-serve-nation": to be born again seven times to serve the nation.

Minamoto no Sanetomo's,

> Should it be a world
> Where the mountains crashed
> And the deeps ran dry,
> Could I possess for my Lord
> A double heart!

The priest Gesshō's,

> If it be for my Lord,
> Would I count it a loss—
> Though my body sank deep
> In Satsuma's sea?

Hirano Kuniomi's,

> O that I could die
> Beneath the Emperor's banner,
> Though deserveless of a name!

Umeda Umpin's,

> Thoughtless am I of my being,
> In the singleness of heart that thinks
> For the reign of His Majesty!

Loyalty is realized through the people's constant attention to duties and through faithful devotion to their pursuits. As graciously manifested in the Imperial Rescript on Education: not only to offer oneself courageously to the State, should occasion arise; but also to be filial to one's parents, affectionate to one's brothers and sisters, to be harmonious as husbands and wives, to be true as friends, to bear oneself in modesty and moderation, to extend one's benevolence to all, to pursue learning and to cultivate arts, and thereby to develop intellectual faculties and to perfect moral powers; furthermore, to advance public good and to promote common interests, always to respect the Constitution and to observe the laws, etc., are one and all accounted for by our response to the great august Will and our respectful support for His Majesty's diffusion of His enterprises, and all constitute the Way of loyalty. Tachibana no Moribe relates in the *Taimon Zakki*:

The general public are ready to look upon serving at the Imperial Palace alone as service; but beneath this shining Sun and Moon,[14] is there anyone that does not serve the Emperor? Beginning with the Gracious Personage who headeth the Government officials right down to the lowest—though there may be differences of high and low—since every one of them is a servant of the Sovereign, to write a thing is for His Majesty, to cure an illness is for His Majesty, to cultivate a field is for His Majesty, and to trade is for His Majesty. But since the lowly are very far separated from His Majesty, they cannot serve the Emperor to the extent of exercising their sympathies for the general public by serving close to the Emperor.

Verily, for those engaged in government, those engaged in industries, those that have dedicated themselves to education or scholastic pursuits, for them to devote themselves to their various fields, is the Way of loyalty to sustain the prosperity of the Imperial Throne, and is by no means a personal Way.

This fact is evidenced by what the Emperor Meiji says in [two of] his poems:

> Lieth Our strength
>   In the people's strength
> That strive to the utmost
>   Each in his sphere.

> Might we serve our Land,
>   Each in our allotted sphere,
> Learning the Way our hearts
>   Should take.

It is the duty of a subject and the noble concern of the Japanese to stand in the deep knowledge that to do one's duty means in effect to sustain the Emperor's great august enterprises, with diligence exercised in perfect accord with the Imperial Will expressed in the words:

---

[14]I.e., throughout the whole country.

In private affairs, with prudence and frugality, carry on your daily duties, and order your mode of living; in public affairs, do not pay attention solely to individual benefits, but devote yourselves to the common weal, and thereby give heed to the welfare, peace, and prosperity of the State, and to social well-being.[15]

FILIAL PIETY

In our country filial piety is a Way of the highest importance. Filial piety originates with one's family as its basis, and in its larger sense has the nation for its foundation. Filial piety directly has for its object one's parents, but in its relationship toward the Emperor finds a place within loyalty.

The basis of the nation's livelihood is, as in the Occident, neither the individual nor husband and wife. It is the home. The domestic life does not consist in a lateral relationship, such as between husband and wife or elder brother and younger brother; but that which forms its root is a dimensional[16] relationship between parent and child. The harmonious merging under the head of a family, in line with our national entity, of a united group of relatives that come together and help each other with the relationship between parent and child for its basis is our nation's home. Consequently, a family is not a body of people established for profit, nor is it anything founded on such a thing as individual or correlative love. Founded on a natural relationship of begetting and being begotten, it has reverence and affection as its kernel; and is a place where everybody, from the very moment of his birth, is entrusted with his destiny.

The life of a family in our country is not confined to the present life of a household of parents and children, but beginning with the distant ancestors, is carried on eternally by the descendants. The present life of a family is a link between the past and the future,

---

[15]Part of the Imperial Rescript on the Promotion of the National Spirit, November 10, 1923, or the twelfth year of Taishō. The Japanese name for the Rescript is *Kokumin Seishin Sakkō ni Kansuru Shōsho.*

[16]Or, cubic, solid; used in a geometrical sense.

and while it carries over and develops the objectives of the ancestors, it hands them over to its descendants. Herein also lies the reason why since of old a family name has been esteemed in our country. A family name is an honor to a household built up by one's ancestors, so that to stain this may be looked upon not only as a personal disgrace but as a disgrace to a family that has come down in one line linking the past, present, and future. Accordingly, the announcing of one's real name[17] by a knight who has gone out to the battlefield was in the nature of an oath to fight bravely by speaking of one's ancestors and their achievements, so as not to cast a slur on the name of an esteemed family.

Again, since olden times, there have existed such things as family codes, family precepts, and family customs, and these things have been handed down to and developed by one's offspring; and heirlooms have been prized and preserved as symbols of a household's successions; while by the nation as a whole ancestral tablets have been solemnly taken over. Such things as these show that the basis of the nation's life is in the family and that the family is the training ground for moral discipline based on natural sympathies. Thus, the life of a household is not a thing confined to the present, but is an unbroken chain that passes through from ancestor to offspring. In our country, consequently, importance is laid on the succession of a family, and legally, too, there is established a system of succession to the heirship. The fact that at present there is only inheritance but no succession to heirship in the Occident illustrates the fact that a household in the Occident and that in our country are fundamentally different.

The relationship between parent and child is a natural one, and therein springs the affection between parent and child. Parent and child are a continuation of one chain of life; and since parents are the source of the children, there spontaneously arises toward the children a tender feeling to foster them. Since children are expan-

---

[17]These six words represent *nanori,* an interesting custom of early feudal Japan.

sions of parents, there springs a sense of respect, love for, and indebtedness toward, parents. Since ancient times, as regards relations between parents and children, poems, legends, and historical facts, portraying parents' affection for their children and children's respect for their parents, are exceedingly numerous. In the *Mannyōshū* there is a poem that tells of the love of one Yamanoe no Okura for his child:

> If I eat a melon, it reminds me of my child.
> If I eat a chestnut, it reminds me of my child all the
> more. Whence does it come?
> It rests over my eyes, and I cannot slumber in peace.
> *Hanka*[18]
> Oh, there's nought excels my gem of a child—
> Gold, silver, or gem though it be!

This poem expresses aptly, though briefly, a love that truly thinks of a child. Also, in a poem which Okura composed lamenting the death of his child Furuhi, too, there is seen an expression of an ardent love of a parent for his child:

> He could not know the way.
> So tender of years is he—
> Messenger of the shades, I pray,
> Carry him through on your back.

And the fond respect of a child for its parents is well expressed in poems such as those of Sakimori.[19]

LOYALTY AND FILIAL PIETY AS ONE

Filial piety in our country has its true characteristics in its perfect conformity with our national entity by heightening still further the relationship between morality and nature. Our country is a great

---

[18]A short 31-syllable *tanka* appended to a long *uta*. This *tanka* happens to be appended to the preceding *uta*.

[19]The warriors sent to defend the western frontier in the time of the *Mannyōshū*.

family nation, and the Imperial Household is the head family of
the subjects and the nucleus of national life. The subjects revere
the Imperial Household, which is the head family, with the tender
esteem [they have] for their ancestors; and the Emperor loves his
subjects as his very own.[20] The words in the august will left by the
Emperor Yūryaku [A.D. 457-479], which says: "Though righteousness may in effect be [between] sovereign and subject, affection is
bound up between father and child," bespeak the great august Will
of the successive Emperors. That is to say, the relationship between
sovereign and subject is public[21] and bound with righteousness;
and what he states is that it does not end solely in mere righteousness but that it is bound with sympathies similar to those between
father and child. "Public [ōyake][22] as opposed to "private" [wata-
kushi] signifies the court[23] and means "nation," namely, "house."

Since our ancestors rendered assistance to the spreading of Imperial enterprises by the successive Emperors, for us to show loyalty
to the Emperor is in effect a manifestation of the manners and
customs of our ancestors; and this is why we show filial piety to
our forefathers. In our country there is no filial piety apart from
loyalty, and filial piety has loyalty for its basis. The logic of the
unity of loyalty and filial piety based on national entity herein shines
forth beautifully. Yoshida Shōin says in his *Shiki Shichisoku*:[24]

The Sovereign careth for the well-being of his subjects, and so inher-
iteth the enterprises of the Imperial Ancestors. The subjects manifest
loyalty toward the Emperor, and so inherit the will of their fathers. It is
only in our country that sovereign and subject are united, and that
loyalty and filial piety converge.

---

[20]Another word for "subjects," *sekishi,* is here used, which carries with it
an idea of endearment, frequently translated as "children."

[21]*Oh-yake;* public; open; official; formal.

[22]Here represented entirely in *kana.*

[23]The *furigana* reading for the ideographs for "big house" is again given
as *ōyake;* it may also be written with the ideographs for "public house";
both may stand for "government" as well as "court."

[24]The Seven Rules of Morale.

And this is a most appropriate statement on the oneness of the Way of loyalty and filial piety.

In China, too, importance is laid on filial duty, and they say that it is the source of a hundred deeds. In India, too, gratitude to parents is taught. But their filial piety is not of a kind related to or based on the nation. Filial piety is a characteristic of Oriental morals; and it is in its convergence with loyalty that we find a characteristic of our national morals, and this is a factor without parallel in the world. Accordingly, that which has lost the essential points of these fundamentals cannot be our national filial piety. Such things as the announcing of one's name[25] by a knight by way of declaring that his house finds its source in the Imperial Household, and the tracing of the relationship of family codes and family teachings to the Imperial Household as their remote source, are to be looked upon as traceable to the very same reasons.

The poem by Sakura Azumao which runs:

> Precious are my parents that gave me birth,
> So that I might serve His Majesty.

shows that when filial piety is elevated to loyalty, then for the first time it becomes filial piety. The offering of their two sons for the nation by General Nogi and his wife, even counting it an honor to the family, is a manifestation of a mind [which looks upon] the family and the country as a unit[26] and loyalty and filial piety as one. Thus, the hearts of the subjects that render service through the Way of loyalty and filial piety as one, in uniting with the Emperor's great august heart of benevolence, reap the fruits of concord between the Sovereign and his subjects, and is the basic power of our nation's endless development.

Verily, loyalty and filial piety as one is the flower of our national entity, and is the cardinal point of our people's morals. Hence, national entity forms not only the foundation of morality but of

---

[25]*Nanori*. See note 17, above.
[26]Literally, "one body."

all branches of such things as politics, economics, and industry. Accordingly, the great Way of loyalty and filial piety as one must be made manifest in all practical fields of these national activities and the people's lives. We subjects must strive all the more in loyalty and filial piety for the real manifestation of the immense and endless national entity.

IV

Harmony and Truth

HARMONY

When we trace the marks of the facts of the founding of our country and the progress of our history, what we always find there is the spirit of harmony. Harmony is a product of the great achievements of the founding of the nation, and is the power behind our historical growth; while it is also a humanitarian Way inseparable from our daily lives. The spirit of harmony is built on the concord of all things.[1] When people determinedly count themselves as masters and assert their egos, there is nothing but contradictions and the setting of one against the other; and harmony is not begotten. In individualism it is possible to have coöperation, compromise, sacrifice, etc., so as to regulate and mitigate this contradiction and the setting of one against the other; but after all there exists no true harmony. That is, the society of individualism is clashes between a people and a people,[2] and history may be all looked upon as that of class wars. Social structure and political systems in such a society, and the theories of sociology, political science, statecraft, etc., which are their logical manifestations, are essentially different from those of our country which makes harmony its fundamental Way. Herein indeed lies the reason why the ideologies of our nation are different from those of the nations of the West.

Harmony as of our nation is not a mechanical concert of independent individuals of the same level that has its starting point in [cold] knowledge, but a great harmony that holds itself together by having the parts within the whole through actions that fit the parts. Hence therein is practiced mutual respectful love and obedience, endearment and fostering. This is not a mere compromise or concord of mechanical or homogeneous things; but is [a thing]—

---

[1]Or, the whole creation.
[2]Literally, "ten thousand men against ten thousand men."

with all things having their characteristics, mutually different and yet manifesting their characteristics, that is, manifesting the essential qualities through the parts—that thus harmonize with the monastic world.[3] That is, harmony as in our nation is a great harmony of individuals who, by giving play to their characteristics, and through difficulties, toil and labor, converge into one. Because of characteristics and difficulties, this harmony becomes all the greater and its substance rich. Again, in this way individualities are developed, special characteristics become beautiful, and at the same time even enhance the development and well-being of the whole. Indeed, harmony in our nation is not a half-measure harmony, but a great, practical harmony that manifests itself with freshness in step with the development of [all] things.

THE MARTIAL SPIRIT

And then, this harmony is clearly seen also in our nation's martial spirit. Our nation is one that holds *bushidō* in high regard, and there are shrines deifying warlike[4] spirits. At the time of the issuing of an Imperial mandate commanding to make and to consolidate,[5] to begin with, a heavenly halberd made of a precious stone was granted; on the occasion of the descent to earth of the Imperial Grandchild, too, the affair was carried out peacefully by a martial deity; and also on the occasion of the Emperor Jimmu's august expedition to the East martial spirit was exercised. But this martial spirit is not [a thing that exists] for the sake of itself but for the sake of peace,[6] and is what may be called a sacred[7] martial spirit. Our martial spirit does not have for its objective the killing of men, but the giving of life to men. This martial spirit is that which tries to give life to all things, and is not that which destroys. That is to

---

[3]*Ichinyo no sekai,* a Buddhist term.
[4]Literally, "rough."
[5]I.e., the creation.
[6]Or, harmony.
[7]Literally, "divine, godly."

say, it is a strife which has peace at its basis with a promise to raise and to develop; and it gives life to things through its strife. Here lies the martial spirit of our nation. War, in this sense, is not by any means intended for the destruction, overpowering, or subjugation of others; and it should be a thing for the bringing about of great harmony, that is, peace,[8] doing the work of creation by following the Way.

MUSUBI[9] AND HARMONY

Through such harmony as this are our national creations and developments materialized. *Musubi* is "creation," and it is in effect a manifestation of the power of harmony. His Augustness Izanagi no Mikoto and Her Augustness Izanami no Mikoto in harmony gave birth to the deities and our Land. This in short is great *musubi*. *Musubi* comes from *musu*. *Musu,* as in *koke musu* [moss grows],[10] means the generating of things. When things harmonize [together] there is *musubi*. Hence, through harmony and mutual fellowship between sovereign and subject is a nation created and developed. The various national reforms and improvements, too, which are a problem of the day, must be [in line with] this *musubi* which is brought about by harmony. This must mean the correcting of wrongs by examining [oneself] in the light of our national entity under the august grace of the Emperor and the lively bringing forth of new fruits through great harmony.

HARMONY BETWEEN "GOD" AND MAN

Furthermore, in our country one finds harmony between "God" and man. When we compare this with the relationship between "God" and man in Western countries, we notice a great difference.

[8]These two are almost literal translations of *tai-wa* and *hei-wa,* the second word being the usual expression for "peace."

[9]This is a Shinto word of a highly mystical nature whose meaning will be best gathered from reading the paragraph.

[10]It is to be noted that the national anthem ends, *koke no musu made,* which means, "until [at length] moss grows."

Such things as the expulsion and punishment by God and His severe chastisement, which appear in Occidental mythology, differ widely from our nation's stories handed down since of old; and here we find a great difference between the relationship between "God" and man as of our nation and that as of Western nations. This is a thing clearly seen also in our nation's religious rites[11] and [Shinto] prayers;[12] and in our country, "God" is not a terrible being, but One that extendeth divine help and is fondly esteemed and [toward whom] gratitude is felt. And the relationship between "God" and man is extremely intimate.

HARMONY BETWEEN MAN AND NATURE

Again, this harmony is also seen in the most intimate relationship between man and nature. Our country is surrounded by the sea, excels in mountains, [is blessed with] limpid waters, and with [happy] changes in the four seasons, and has natural features not found in other countries. These beautiful natural features were brought to birth by the heavenly deities together with the [many] deities; and though they be things on which one may set one's affection they are [certainly] not objects of fear. It is here that our national trait to love nature is begotten and the harmony between man and nature is established. India, for instance, is overpowered by her natural features, and in the Occident one senses the subjugation of nature by man, and there is not found a deep harmony between man and nature as in our country. On the contrary, our people are in constant harmony with nature. In literature, too, many are the poems that sing of this harmonious mind toward nature, and deep love toward nature forms the principal theme of our poetry. This is not confined to the world of literature; but in our daily lives, too, nature and human existence harmonize. If we look at the events of the year according to the four seasons mentioned in *Kuji*

[11]*Saishi.*
[12]*Norito.* The word represents addresses to deities.

Kongen[13] and others, we see the exquisite harmony since of old between human existence and nature. The New Year's functions, needless to say, and the Dolls' Festival in March are functions that befit the natural [beauties] of spring, and the Chrysanthemum Festival also befits the greeting of autumn. In our country, where the transitions between the seasons are clearly marked, this harmony of nature and human existence is especially and beautifully vivid. Besides, in family crests zoological and botanical [designs] are much used, and in attire, architectural objects, and gardens, too, natural beauty is effectively used. This intimate, single relationship between nature and man, also, finds its source in our original, national ideology in which man and nature enjoy coalescent intimacy.

MUTUAL HARMONY AMONG THE PEOPLE

This harmonious spirit is also widely realized in the life of the nation. In our country, under a unique family system, parent and child and husband and wife live together, supporting and helping each other. In the Imperial Rescript on Education the Emperor Meiji graciously says: "Husbands and wives, be harmonious." And this harmony between husband and wife must merge into and become one with: "Be filial to your parents." That is, a family must be a place where there prospers a well-merged, united harmony in the union of a vertical harmony between parents and children and of a lateral harmony among husbands and wives, brothers and sisters.

Going a step further, this harmony must also be made to materialize in communal life. Those serving in Government offices as well as those working in firms must follow this Way of harmony. In each community there are those who take the upper places while there are those who work below them. Through each one fulfilling his portion is the harmony of a community obtained. To fulfill one's part means to do one's appointed task with the utmost faithfulness

[13]A book written in the Oh-ei "Period" (*nengō*), 1394-1427.

each in his own sphere; and by this means do those above receive help[14] from inferiors, and inferiors are loved by superiors; and in working together harmoniously is beautiful concord manifested and creative work carried out.

This applies both to the community and to the State. In order to bring national harmony to fruition, there is no way but for every person in the nation to do his allotted duty and to exalt it. Those in high positions, low positions, rich, and poor, in or out of official life, those holding public or private positions, as well as those engaged in agriculture, industries, trade, etc., should not stand aloof one from the other by being taken up with themselves, but should not fail to make harmony their foundation.

In short, in our country, differences of opinion or of interests that result from one's position easily [merge] into one through our unique great harmony which springs from the same source. In all things strife is not the final goal, but harmony; all things do not end with destruction, but bear fruit in their fulfillment. Herein is the great spirit of our nation. In this manner is every progress and development seen in our nation carried out. Shōtoku Taishi [A.D. 572-621][15] sets forth in his *Code of Laws in Seventeen Chapters*:[16]

Count it sacred to have bonds of harmony, and make it thy principle not to have strifes. Every man is influenced by his circumstances, and few be they that have divined the truth. As a consequence, a person obeyeth not his ruler or father, but quarreleth with his neighbors. Howbeit, when superiors and inferiors understand each other in their conversations, the logic of a thing naturally becometh clear. What is there that cannot be done?

And Shōtoku Taishi said this to expound this great spirit of harmony as it [exists] in our country.

---

[14]In the sense of "support."
[15]Second son of the Emperor Yōmei (A.D. 586-587), and one of the great figures in Japanese history, especially in connexion with Buddhism.
[16]Promulgated in A.D. 604.

SOVEREIGN AND SUBJECTS IN ONE

In our country, Sovereign and subjects have from of old been spoken of as being one, and the entire nation, united in mind and acting in full coöperation, have shown forth the beauties of this oneness with the Emperor as their centre. The august virtues of the Emperor and the duties of the subjects converge and unite into a beautiful harmony. The Emperor Nintoku [A.D. 313-399] has said:

> The poverty of Our subjects meaneth in effect Our poverty. The opulence of Our subjects meaneth in effect Our opulence.

Again, the Emperor Kameyama [A.D. 1260-1274], on the occasion of the Mongolian Invasion, offered a written prayer at the Ise Shrine and did pray: "Let Our own Person bear the national crisis!" Again, His Majesty the Present Emperor says in his Imperial Rescript issued on the occasion of his enthronement:

> When Our Imperial Ancestors founded the nation and reigned over Their subjects, They counted the nation Their family and looked upon Their subjects as Their own children. The successive Emperors one and all extended Their benevolent rule and the entire nation showed reverence and loyalty to the Sovereign following the ways of old, the Sovereign and subjects expressing mutual sympathy, and being united in one. This is the excellence of Our national entity and it must abide together with Heaven and Earth.

In this are we able to behold an unadulterated manifestation of the supreme harmony in [His Majesty's] sharing, in the oneness with the people, of their pleasures and hardships. Then again, the burden of the poem:

> What loss count I to lay down my life
> For my Lord and for the world—
> Since my life's worth sacrifice![17]

---

[17]By Munenaga Shinnō (A.D. 1312-1385), fourth son of the Emperor Go-Daigo.

bespeaks the climax of harmony in the sacrifice of the life of a subject for the Emperor.

It is when this harmonious spirit of our nation is spread abroad throughout the world and every race and State, with due attention to its appointed duties, gives full play to its own characteristics, that true world peace and its progress and prosperity are realized.

TRUTH

A true heart is the most genuine thing in the spirit of man. Man has his basis of life in truth, through truth he becomes one with all things, gives life to and harmonizes with all things.[18]

As regards truth, Kamo no Mabuchi [A.D. 1697-1769][19] and Fujitani Mitsue [A.D. 1768-1823][20] expounded it, laying special weight on it. True words are in effect true deeds.[21] Words and deeds must meet in truth; that is, what has been spoken must be put into practice without fail. In the very source which comprises this "language" and "deed" lies truth. Mitsue divides this heart into *hitoegokoro, hitaburu kokoro,* and *magokoro. Hitoegokoro* is an egoistic heart, while *hitaburu kokoro* is a heart that behaves in a stubborn way. Neither of these can be called a perfect heart. *Magokoro* is a heart which does not override moral bounds by following its own wishes. Such a heart is in effect deeds, words, and actions, and is free of encumbrances, not being enslaved by any one deed or thing. That is to say, it is a genuine heart and a genuine deed that is freed of self. Indeed, truth melts and unites together all things, releasing them of encumbrances. Truth manifested in art becomes beauty, and as morality becomes goodness, and in knowledge, veracity. It is to be noted that truth exists in the source

---

[18]Or, the whole creation.

[19]Or, Kamo Mabuchi. A son of a *kan-nushi* of Kamo Temple in Tōtōmi.

[20]One of the best-known members of a renowned family of *literati.*

[21]The *furigana,* or given *kana* readings, for both these character combinations read *makoto,* i.e. "truth."

which gives birth to beauty, goodness, and veracity. Thus, truth is in turn what is generally spoken of as a bright, clean, honest heart, that is to say, *Seimeishin* [clear, bright heart],[22] and this forms the basis of our national spirit.

Since truth is the fountainhead of reason, will, and emotion; knowledge, pity, and courage may be looked upon as manifestations of truth. Our national Way by no means counts it sufficient to have courage alone. To let courage alone run away with oneself means courage of a low quality, so that both courage and pity need go together. Hence, in order to manifest courage and pity there must needs be knowledge. That means, these three things meet as one truth, and through truth these three work together efficaciously.

In the Imperial Rescript Granted to the Men of the Forces, the Emperor Meiji points out five virtues, which are fealty, etiquette, chivalry, fidelity, and frugality; and declares by way of advice how it is necessary to achieve this [ideal] with one's whole heart.

The five preceding Articles are things which a soldier must not for a moment neglect. Wherefore, in order to carry this out, what is vital is a single, unsullied heart. The five Articles represent the spirit of the men of our Forces, and this single, unsullied heart is in turn the spirit of the five Articles. Unless the heart be unsullied, however good one's words or deeds may be, they are all nothing but superficial ornaments which are of no use whatever. If the heart be sincere, is there anything that cannot be accomplished!

Furthermore, actions carried out with sincerity are indeed genuine actions. Genuine words, genuine actions. Words that can be turned into actions are indeed genuine words. Our national idea of words has its basis here; so that as for words that cannot be turned into action, one must be discreet and not utter them. This is the heart of man as it should be. Words full of truth are in effect words [of the soul]; and such words are inherent with great deeds, that is, have infinitely strong power, and speak with an endless breadth.

---

[22]There is much juggling with Chinese characters and words.

It is this the *Mannyōshū* speaks of when it says that Japan is "a Land where words [of the soul] flourish." Hence, one hears, too, the expression, "A Land of the deities which is free from the strife of words." This on the surface looks inconsistent, but in reality it is not so. Once a thing is said, one must by all means put it into practice; so that one should not utter at random words that cannot be followed out by actions. Accordingly, once a thing is stated, it must by every means be practiced. Nay, if genuine words or genuine words [of the soul],[23] they must of necessity be put into practice. Thus, at the roots of words that can be turned into actions there is truth. There must be no self in truth. When one speaks and acts, utterly casting oneself aside, there indeed is truth, and there indeed shines truth.

---

[23]*Kotodama;* lit. word + spirit. This is a euphonic and honorific word for "word," appearing several times in this section, and carries with it an idea of refinement and mystery.

BOOK II

THE MANIFESTATION OF
OUR NATIONAL ENTITY IN HISTORY

I

The Spirit That Runs Through History

THE TRUE MEANING OF OUR NATIONAL HISTORY

Our national history is a history that rolls ahead as an unfolding of the single course of the great spirit of the founding of the nation, which has extended to the present day. In history there is a spirit that runs through it together with the changes and the transitions of the times. In our history the spirit of the founding of the nation abides majestic, and becomes clearer and clearer; so that historical developments are in short the unfolding of the spirit of the founding of the Empire, and are the creation and development of eternal life. Yet, in other countries, the life cords of the nation are cut off through revolutions and downfalls, so that the spirit of the founding of the nation is disrupted and dies off, giving birth to another national history. Hence, we do not find a spirit of the founding of a nation continuing incorruptible and imperishable throughout their history. Accordingly, when seeking for something that runs through the history of another nation, there is no other way than to set up something in the form of a general rule based on abstract reason. This is why historical views in the West transcend the nation. In our country, history cannot be understood without having for its basis the great spirit of the founding of the Empire and an unbroken line of Imperial rule. Kitabatake Chikafusa [A.D. 1293-1354][1] in an apt statement on the incomparable nature of our Imperial line says in the opening passage of *Jin-nō Shōtōki:*

Japan is a Land of the gods. Our Imperial Ancestor for the first time set the foundation of the nation, and the Sun Deity for ever handeth on the Imperial Throne. This is a thing existing only in our country and without parallel in foreign lands. This is why we call it a Land of the gods.

---

[1] Came of a family of *daimyō.*

In Japanese history we may come across reformations, but revolutions are nil; the spirit of the founding of the Empire has continued throughout history unbroken to the present time, and is a power that will transcend the morrow. Accordingly, in our country, national history begins and ends with national entity, and is a self-expression of [this] national entity.

The august spirit in which His Augustness Izanagi no Mikoto and Her Augustness Izanami no Mikoto made and consolidated [the Land], and in which Amaterasu Ohmikami founded the Empire—which are things already referred to—has been realised in the great august Will of the successive Emperors in the governing of their country. That is, the august spirit of the Oracle is a thing that runs through the Imperial proclamations issued by the successive Emperors; and innovations or reformations that appear in our history do the work of manifesting the right by returning to the very fountain head of history. Thus, we subjects, following this great principle, have assisted the great [august] enterprises, shaping our resplendent history.

DEDICATION OF THE LAND BY OHKUNINUSHI NO KAMI

According to the *Kojiki* and the *Nihon-shoki,* prior to the descent of the Imperial Grandson on the Land of Fresh Rice-ears of Luxurious Reed Plains,[2] the Grandson despatched two deities, Kashima and Katori, to Izumo; and upon delivering the Oracle of Amaterasu Ohmikami to the Deity Master-of-Great-Land,[3] the Deity Master-of-Great-Land together with his son Kotoshironushi no Kami obeyed the Imperial command and swore allegiance, dedicated the Land, and separated himself from governmental affairs. This is a vital example of lending a hand in a great enterprise, and on the occasion the Deity Master-of-Great-Land did declare in his oath:

What my two children have said does not differ from my ideas. This *Ashihara no Nakatsu-Kuni* I will return in perfect compliance with what

[2]Toyoashihara no Mizuho no Kuni.
[3]Ohkuninushi no Kami.

thou sayest. Only, I pray thee build my dwelling with thick pillars and high crossbeams,[4] like unto the Palace of the august son of the heavenly deities in the Land over which the august son of the heavenly deities reigneth. Then would I protect this Land, giving attention to every little thing, when I depart to the Land of the Shades. Again, as for my one hundred and eighty children, not one should prove disobedient, since the deity Yaekotoshironushi no Kami will serve the [many] deities on every hand.

Thus, the Deity Master-of-Great-Land, who had dedicated the Land, had a magnificent palace builded for him by [Amaterasu] Ohmi-kami and was treated with much hospitality. Therefore, the Deity Master-of-Great-Land is today deified in the Grand Shrine of Izumo, and has come to guard our land for ever and ever. It is thus that we see the beginning of the great spirit of the restoration of the Imperial rule in the Meiji Reformation, when the Government, begun by Minamoto Yoritomo, fell, and the administration was returned whole to the Court through the restoration of the administrative authority to the Throne toward the end of the Tokugawa regime and the retrocession of feuds against the Emperor that followed.

EXPANSION OF IMPERIAL ENTERPRISES BY THE EMPEROR JIMMU

The Emperor Jimmu's expedition to the East extended over a long period, and His Majesty fought against many hardships. And although he met with the terrible grief of losing his Imperial elder brother Itsuse no Mikoto, he would not yield to grief, but finally achieved his great undertaking through his august convictions and will to expand the Imperial enterprises as an august son of the heavenly deities. The traditions of the mythological age and our national history that has followed show that through such ceaseless efforts of the successive Emperors every obstacle has been surmounted, Imperial enterprises expanded, a good and beautiful nation built up, and that the splendor of our national entity is on the

---

[4]Crossbeams on the roof of a Shinto shrine.

rise. In the edict issued by the Emperor Jimmu when he chose the
Land of Kashiwabara in Yamato as the site for the capital, the
Emperor says:

When a sage establisheth rules, the moral codes are appropriate to
the times. If it prove a blessing to the people, how should it be at vari-
ance with the deeds of the Emperor! Wherefore, We hope to ascend the
Throne and, after clearing the forests and building Our palace, to rule
over Our subjects. On the one hand, We shall respond to the august
graciousness seen in the granting of the Land by the Spirit of the Imperial
Ancestress, and on the other, We shall encourage the mind of Our Imperial Grandchild who cultivated righteousness. Then, We hope to establish a capital, from which to unite the whole realm, placing the whole
world under one roof.[5] Is this not a good thing to do?

So saying, he has made clear the spirit in which the heavenly deities
bestowed the Land and the spirit in which the Imperial Grandchild
cultivated righteousness. This great august mind is clearly seen
both in the fact of the founding of the Empire and in the Oracle,
which are things we have already referred to; and the diffusion of
the Imperial Grandchild's august mind to cultivate the right is made
evident by the sacred administration of the Emperors that have succeeded the Emperor Jimmu. This is accounted for by the fact that
the Imperial Ancestors have founded the Empire on a basis broad
and everlasting and have deeply and firmly implanted virtue.[6] The
Emperor Jimmu ascended the Throne with such a deep august
mind as this, and with a great spirit [which had in mind] the uniting of the whole realm and the mantling of the whole world. Again,
in the fourth spring of his reign, the Emperor said in an edict:

The Spirit of Our Imperial Ancestress descended from heaven, illu-

---

[5]From this passage is derived the expression *Hakkō Ichiu,* a philosophy
of universal brotherhood which has defied a satisfactory explanation.

[6]This passage forms a part of the Imperial Rescript on Education issued
by the Emperor Meiji, a greater part of which appears in Book I.

mined and helped Our Person. Now have all the rebels been subdued and
peace reigneth throughout the whole Land. Wherefore, it would be good
to hold divine services to the heavenly deity and to practise filial piety.

And built on Mount Tomi a court of worship, deifying his Imperial
Ancestress, the heavenly goddess, and so showed sincerity by paying
attention to the root and source [of things].

THE EMPEROR SUJIN'S REVERENCE FOR
THE DEITIES OF HEAVEN AND EARTH

Later in our history, the Emperor Sujin [B.C. 97-30] enshrined
Amaterasu Ohmikami in the village called Kasanui in Yamato,
and the Emperor Suinin [B.C. 29--A.D. 70] built the Grand Shrine
of Ise by the River Isuzu in Ise, which things are manifestations of
the great august mind which holds the Imperial Ancestress in
reverence. Furthermore, such facts as the Emperor Sujin's diffusion
of culture by dispatching military governors of the four provinces,
levying taxes and setting up public duties by establishing laws of
taxation, and his constructing of ponds and ditches [for irrigation],
all show his inheritance of the august spirit of the Imperial Ancestors and his taking over and handing down of the Imperial enterprises and his encouragement given thereto.

REFORM OF THE TAIKA ERA

The Reform of the Taika Era was carried out through help
accorded the Emperor Kōtoku [A.D. 645-654] by Prince Naka no
Oh-e[7] with a view to correcting the abuses of the clan system. In
this Reform, the Emperor adapted a Chinese ideology according to
which [the ideal] is for the monarch to take the reins of government, assimilated the good points of institutions existing in the Sui
and T'ang Dynasties, and put an end to the abuses of civilian rights
and owning of lands together with the people on them by clansmen,

[7]Became the Emperor Tenchi (A.D. 662-671).

doing away especially with the highhanded ways of the Soga Clan.[8]
And the great spirit of this Reform finds its origin in the clarification of [the meaning of] great moral obligations between Sovereign
and subject set forth in Shōtoku Taishi's *Code of Laws in Seventeen
Chapters*. The Emperor Kōtoku caused Prince Naka no Oh-e to
take definite steps to instill this spirit of Shōtoku Taishi in the world
of politics and institutions.

The institution of twelve rankings established during the reign
of the Empress Suiko [A.D. 593-628] clarified [the meaning of] the
great principle of giving the first place to the Throne and the great
august spirit of nondiscrimination among the people, and by this
the Empress points out how everybody should attain his aim and
assist the Imperial enterprises. Again, in the *Code of Laws in Seventeen Chapters* Her Majesty clearly points out the spirit of concord
and how a nation cannot have two sovereigns, elucidating the royal
Way [in the relation] between Sovereign and subject and in public
and private life. A glance into the accomplishments of the Taika
Reform, which is [marked by] this great principle of [relation be-
tween] Sovereign and subject and the august spirit of nondiscrimination among the people, brings before us Prince Naka no Oh-e's
address in reply to a gracious speech by His Majesty [the Emperor
Kōtoku], which says:

In heaven there are not two Suns, and in a country there are not two
monarchs. Hence, the Emperor is the only one that should have all the
people serve him throughout the whole realm.

Again, the Emperor [Kōtoku] says by way of a decree to the pro-
vincial officials: "We cannot impoverish Our people by taking commission from them."

Thus, the Reform of the Taika Era saw the restoration of people
and lands belonging to clans and the return of the entire adminis-

---

[8]A powerful family, *gōzoku*, that for several generations occupied the position of *ō-omi* (literally, great subject) in ancient Japan. The characters for
ō-omi are the same as those for *daijin*, minister.

trative power to the Imperial Court; and as a result of the breaking
down of evil practices foreign ideas and institutions received [due]
consideration; and in the Imperial edict issued in the first year of
Taika, His Majesty says: "We ought to govern the realm following
the example set by the noble sovereigns of old." And in the Imperial
edict issued in the third year of Taika he says:

> In the divine ages it was said, "Our child, rule thou [over this Land],"
> and so deigned to charge him. Wherefore, this is a Land, since the begin-
> ning of Heaven and Earth, over which the Emperors do reign . . . Hence,
> [there are those] who put this before or this after a thing[9] [to suit their
> convenience] in governing the Land and the people, without an under-
> standing of these things, at a time when one must now govern in peace,
> following the manner of the divine ages. Today and tomorrow,[10] Im-
> perial edicts shall follow one another.

And in so saying His Majesty set forth the great policy of returning
to the spirit of ancient times which had as its nucleus the Emperor,
who is a humanly manifested deity in keeping with the great significance of the "god-handed" founding of the Empire. Again, the
words of Soga no Ishikawamaro which run: "First of all, enshrine
the deities of heaven and earth, and after that shall the affairs of
administration be surely contrived," are an attempt to follow the
old institution in which religious rites and government were united.
It is where renovations are thus carried out in the spirit of reforms
that take us back to the [good] old ways and where the Imperial
enterprises are diffused, that we see the manifestation of our great
"god-handed" Way.

These renovations were not completed within the Taika Epoch,
but were carried on further into the reign of the Emperor Mommu
[A.D. 697-707]. That is to say, the various laws were put into shape
in the *Ohmiryō*[11] which was followed by the institution of *Taihō-*

---

[9]That is, to govern as one likes without paying any attention to the proper
modes of administration.
[10]I.e., from now on, hereafter, too.
[11]Law code drafted in the second half of the seventh century.

ritsuryō[12] and still further by the revisions made in the Yōrō Period [A.D. 717-724]. The Emperor Temmu [A.D. 673-686] greatly revered the deities of heaven and earth, and set about collocating the annals of ancient happenings and the records of the Emperors' activities to be handed down to future generations. This august spirit and these august enterprises were spoken of from generation to generation, and later resulted in the annals of the *Kojiki* and the compilation of the *Nihon-shoki*.

LOYALTY OF WAKE NO KIYOMARO[13]

We have already related how the malignant arrogance of the Soga Clan was removed and how a return was made to the great Way which properly belongs to our country. But in the reign of the Empress Shōtoku [A.D. 765-769] the Priest Dōkyō wielded power and authority over the Government and the people and came to harbor inordinate ambition. However, Wake no Kiyomaro, in compliance with an Imperial order, received the injunctions of the deities [at a Shinto shrine], and stood up fearlessly and crushed the evil designs with a resolute spirit, forgetful of dangers to his own person. The august injunctions of the deities which Kiyomaro reported by way of a reply appear in the *Shoku-Nihongi*:[14]

In our country the duties of the Sovereign and the subjects have been determined since the dawn of our history. For a subject to become a ruler is a thing as yet unknown. Without fail set upon the Throne one who is of the Imperial Blood. Be ye certain and quick to clear away any malignant person.

---

[12]Or, *Taihō-ryōritsu*, a code of laws promulgated in the first year of Taihō (A.D. 701).

[13]A.D. 733-799. One of an ancient family which played a prominent part during the eighth and ninth centuries.

[14]Historical records covering a period of 95 years (A.D. 697-792), or from the first year of the reign of the Emperor Mommu to the tenth year of the Emperor Kammu's reign.

In this manner did Kiyomaro guard the Imperial Throne coeval
with heaven and earth and fulfill the mission of sustaining the prosperity of the Throne, and later the Emperor Kōmei [A.D. 1847-
1867][15] gave him the divine title of Go-ō Daimyōjin.[16]

ESTABLISHMENT OF THE KAMAKURA GOVERNMENT

Minamoto Yoritomo's [A.D. 1147-1199][17] installing of *Shugo* and
Jitō,[18] after his destruction of the Heike family,[19] by petitioning the
Throne by which means he carried out the control of lands through-
out the whole country, and his setting up of the shogunate govern-
ment by seizing the reins of government, are indeed administrative
abnormalities that run counter to our national entity. Hence, the
Emperor Meiji declared in his Imperial Rescript Granted to the
Men of the Forces, concerning the shogunate administration:

Furthermore, it is indeed contrary to our national entity and indeed
in violation of the laws set by Our Imperial Ancestors, and a thing to be
truly ashamed of.

And His Majesty gave admonition, saying,

We desire that there be no more loss of face as that which followed
the establishment of the Kamakura Shogunate.

---

[15]His reign is made significant by the arrival of foreigners which hastened
the overthrow of the Shōgun.

[16]Literally, "Monarch-guarding Great-light-deity."

[17]The first Minamoto Shōgun, and a member of one of the most outstanding families in Japanese history.

[18]Names of official positions of the Kamakura and Muromachi periods,
shugo meaning literally "protector," and *jitō*, "land chief." In A.D. 1185
Minamoto no Yoritomo was granted official sanction to appoint these *shugo*
and *jitō* to every province. This event is significant in that through acquisition
of feudal lordship by a *samurai*, feudalism was instituted.

[19]Or, the Taira family, whose supremacy lasted A.D. 1159-1185. The
Minamoto and Taira families were constantly pitted against each other, and
played such an important part in history, that one of the eras is known as the
Gempei Era, *Gen* being the Japanised Chinese reading for *Minamoto*, and
pei, which is *hei* when alone, standing for *Hei* in *Heike*.

RESTORATION OF THE KEMMU ERA

After the downfall of the Genji,[20] the Regents Hōjō[21] proved themselves even more stubborn in disobeying the Emperor's commands, and in the days of Yoshitoki [A.D. 1163-1224][22] became all the more insolent. Accordingly, the ex-Emperors Go-Toba [A.D. 1186-1198], Tsuchimikado [A.D. 1199-1210], and Juntoku [A.D. 1211-1221] together contrived to overthrow them, so that the direct Imperial rule might be restored. This means that these Emperors acted in the great spirit of bringing about the reëstablishment of the Imperial regime, a spirit that inherits the great policy seen in the founding of the Empire. However, the treachery of the Hōjō during this period was of a most pernicious nature. Nevertheless the august spirit of the three ex-Emperors bore fruit in the reigns of the Emperors Go-Uda [A.D. 1275-1287] and Go-Daigo [A.D. 1319-1338] as the great enterprise of the Restoration of the Kemmu Era [A.D. 1334-1335]. The gracious aspiration of the Imperial Family, at that time, to restore the old ways, following the sacred eras of Engi [A.D. 901-923] and Tenryaku [A.D. 947-957], are witnessed in various writings. Indeed, the Restoration of the Kemmu Era was an antiphon to the Taika Reform, and a sacred enterprise that later in history awoke the Meiji Restoration [A.D. 1868]; and in these things we see the gracious endeavors of the Emperors and princes of the Blood and the assistance of many loyal subjects. That is, among the loyal subjects were such names as Kitabatake Chikafusa [A.D. 1293-1354], Hino Suketomo [died A.D. 1332], Hino Toshimoto, Nitta Yoshisada [A.D. 1301-1338],[23] and Kusunoki Masashige

---

[20]Another name for the Minamoto family.

[21]A family descended from Taira Sadamori, whose members from A.D. 1200-1333 were the actual rulers of the country.

[22]He succeeded his father Hōjō Tokimasa in the office of Shikken, or Regent.

[23]Renowned for capturing Kamakura and putting an end to the Hōjō domination.

[A.D. 1294-1336];[24] and through such men were titanic tasks accomplished. Among these, the achievements of Kusunoki Masashige in particular have long remained with us a pattern. In the *Taiheiki*[25] it has it that

His Majesty commanded to have the bamboo screen lifted high, and ordered Masashige to draw nigh, saying with emotion, "Thou art wholeheartedly in thy loyal battle, in thy meritorious service to carry out immediate justice,"

to which gracious speech Masashige made a solemn reply,

But for Thy benevolence in Thy versatility in letters and arts of war, how shall this unworthy self bring to nought by some little stratagem the siege of so powerful an enemy!

This is truly a manifestation of how self was entirely lost in the loyal spirit of a subject and his deeds, and of obedience to the Emperor's great august Will and the great spirit of the founding of the Empire, and the genuine spirit and actions that spring therefrom. The epitaph on the tombstone in Minatogawa Shrine which reads, "AH! THE GRAVE OF THE LOYAL SUBJECT KUSUNOKI," proclaims to future generations the loyalty of the Kusunoki family.

The great task of the Kemmu Restoration, just referred to, was overthrown by Ashikaga Takauji [A.D. 1305-1358][26] who ignored the principles of justice and struggled to usurp the reins of government. In short, Ashikaga Takauji's high treason and thorough contempt for principles interrupted this great work, as he disregarded our national entity and incited those who thought only of their own gain. Thus, the Emperor's activities in the work of restoration seen in his efforts toward various political reforms and enhancement of

---

[24]One of a family of *daimyō* who together with his eldest son Masatsura fought against the rebel Hōjō Clan which was out to usurp the Throne.

[25]A historical work covering one of the most troubled periods in Japanese history, A.D. 1318-1368.

[26]The first Ashikaga Shōgun.

the spirit of the founding of the Empire were for the second time clothed in darkness. Kitabatake Chikafusa gives way to grief over this matter, saying,

To be born in this Imperial Land and to be loyal and to sacrifice one's life is the Way of the subjects. By no means must one look upon this as a meritorious deed. Howbeit, it is His Majesty's role to encourage one's offspring and to utter words of praise by way of sympathy for those that are left behind. It is not meet that we subordinates should bring up before Him complaints of dissatisfaction. How much more would it mean to endanger oneself to harbor too many hopes when one has rendered no distinguished services worth mentioning? Nevertheless, what a good custom it truly seems to be to watch and learn from the ruts of wheels that have passed before us.

According to the *Taiheiki*, the Emperor Go-Daigo [A.D. 1319-1338] says in his Rescript issued after his death:

There is just one thing that We cannot forget, and that is utterly to destroy all traitors and to have peace throughout the entire realm. After Our demise it would be good to set Daihachi no Miya on the Throne and to have wise knights and loyal subjects lay down plans and, if to the praise of Yoshisuke[27] his offspring do no wrong, to have them rule the realm as loyal subjects.

For sixty ill-fated years covering four reigns beginning with the Emperor Go-Daigo, the Emperors dwelt at Yoshino; and the Emperor Go-Kameyama [A.D. 1372-1392],[28] in his great august desire to console his subjects in their anxiety, abdicated and handed over the Sacred Treasures to the Emperor Go-Komatsu [A.D. 1392-1412]. Kitabatake Chikafusa, who became at this hour the mainstay of the court, wrote the *Jin-nō Shōtōki*[29] in which he expounds "the na-

---

[27]Younger brother of Nitta Yoshisada.

[28]Orthodox date, but through the discovery of another Emperor by the name of Chōkei, whose reign lasted from A.D. 1368 to A.D. 1382, the chronology has been corrected by the Ministry of Education to A.D. 1383-1392.

[29]Historical works covering the period from mythological times up to the reign of the Emperor Go-Murakami (A.D. 1339-1367).

ture of an undisturbed Imperial reign, which must be free of deception," and made the great Way of our nation plain. Chikafusa's magnificent enterprises later became an inspiration for the writing of the *Dai Nihon-shi*[30] and for making the meaning of our national entity quite clear. Then again, the august attitude of Prince Kanenaga [A.D. 1329-1383],[31] a *shōgun* of the Court at Yoshino who went on an expedition to the West, who would by no means allow the national prestige to be disgraced when the nation was menaced by T'ai Tsung of the Ming Dynasty [A.D. 1368-1644], bespoke his strong diplomacy that firmly upheld the spirit of the founding of the Empire; and the difference is truly appalling when this is compared with the attitude of Yoshimitsu and Yoshimasa, descendants of Takauji, who not only forgot their great principle and made light of their moral obligations toward the nation, but as regards the Ming Dynasty did injury to the nation's honor.

Even during the decline in the power of the Court from the Muromachi Era [A.D. 1392-1490] forward, the prosperity of the Imperial Throne, coeval with heaven and earth, remained absolutely immutable, and fruits of reverence toward the Throne were seen even in the midst of national chaos; and this spirit was never lost sight of. Added to this, there was a gradual rise of Shinto philosophy, and the people's reverence toward the Imperial Household manifested itself in a number of beautiful deeds of loyalty.

REVERENCE FOR THE THRONE IN THE EDO PERIOD

In the Kamakura Period [A.D. 1192-1333] the philosophies known as Sōgaku and Zengaku played vital parts in the rise of theses on the moral obligation of subjects toward the Throne and on our national entity, and later had an influence on the achievement of the great work of the Kemmu Restoration. The Tokugawa

---

[30]A great history of Japan comprising 397 volumes.
[31]Son of the Emperor Go-Daigo. Another accepted reading for the characters for Kanenaga is Yasunaga.

Shogunate [A.D. 1603-1868][32] adopted a philosophy called Shushi-gaku [Chu Hsi School], and this scholastic system gave rise to an-other philosophy known as Mitogaku, with the compilation of the *Dai Nihon-shi* playing the main rôle, and this in turn gave birth to Shinto conceptions, and together with the sterling soul of patriot-ism brought to birth Yamazaki Ansai's [A.D. 1618-1682] so-called Sakimon School of philosophy. The works of Ansai's disciples, namely, Asami Keisai's *Seiken Igen*, Yamaga Sokō's *Chūchō Jijitsu*, etc., are, one and all, things that lay emphasis on the great principle of reverence for the Throne, and together with the *Taiheiki*, Rai San-yō's *Nihon Gaishi*, Aizawa Seishisai's *Shinron*, Fujita Tōko's *Kōdōkan Kijutsugi*, as well as treatises by Japanese classical scholars, are literary productions that had tremendous influence on loyalists in the last days of the Tokugawa regime.

A thing that should be looked upon as deserving serious attention alongside with theses on the moral obligation of subjects toward the Throne which appear in the teachings of Confucius [B.C. 551-479] is the systematization and development of Japanese philosophical concepts. The study of Japanese concepts contributed greatly to-ward the advancement of the national spirit, beginning with the research in ancient history and classics, and by laying stress on ancient Ways and the great Way of the deities, on the principle of returning to the revival of the ancient regime. Moto-ori Norinaga's *Kojikiden* is one of the first things to be cited; but Hirata Atsutane and others, too, have given expositions on the great Way of the deities, and have put into practice the results of their researches in Japanese philosophical concepts. Toward the end of the Tokugawa regime, the scholastic systems of Shintoists, Confucianists, and schol-ars in Japanese concepts intermingled with the loyalists; so that the philosophy of reverence for the Throne, together with the doc-trine of alien exclusionism, stirred up the patriots. Indeed, the study of Japanese philosophical concepts made the meaning of our national

---

[32]The Edo Period and the Tokugawa Period are different names for the same period.

entity plain, was an effort toward its enhancement, and became the generative power behind the Meiji Restoration.

That the august virtues of the successive Emperors remain unchanged from one reign to another is a fact we can only mention with awe; and the Emperor Kōmei [A.D. 1847-1867], who expressed great concern over the knotty diplomacy of the last years of the Tokugawa regime, graciously issued Imperial proclamations from time to time to court officials from the Chief Advisor to His Majesty and down, as well as to the Government, and counseled them to preserve the Empire from harm, to do no injustice to the unfinished august activities of the Imperial Ancestors, and also to keep the subjects free from dire distress, and in particular had them report to the Throne regarding vital affairs of the State, and thereby submit matters to the decisions of the Throne. Faced with these difficult times, the lords and knights who feared for the future of the Empire made thorough the defence of the State by carrying out reforms in the government and, in their desire to establish measures against foreign pollution, sought after the Imperial Court and wished to know where the Imperial Will lay, and so came to make known their minds to the Court nobles by coming into contact with them; and thus it was that the Imperial prestige gradually came to make itself felt. Among those who early studied Western learning were those who, with a view to strengthening the national power by assimilating foreign culture, set forth the impossibility of national isolation; but the tide of affairs throughout the whole realm saw the remodeling of the feudal regime and the subsequent exclusion of aliens and the overthrow of the feudal Government, which things came to clash with the opening of the nation's doors and the merging of lords and knights; so that the state of affairs within and without the country became all the more complicated and critical. Indeed, it was evident, once civil war broke out, trouble from without would follow, taking advantage of the situation. The ex-Chief of the Clan of Tosa, Yamanouchi Toyonobu, having learned of this state of affairs, after the Emperor Meiji's accession to the Throne, told the Shōgun Tokugawa Yoshinobu [A.D. 1837-1913],[33] of his belief that the reins of government should be restored to the Throne and that administrative orders should proceed from one source. Yoshinobu, too, had early kept this matter in mind and so petitioned the Emperor to have the administrative authority restored to the Throne, by presenting the following memorial to the Throne on the fourteenth of October in the third year of Keiō [A.D. 1867]:

The powers of the State more than ever do not emanate from a single source. This being the case, rules for governing the country cannot be established; so that if we broke ourselves away from old abuses, restored governmental authority to the Imperial Court, strove to see justice exercised throughout the whole realm, submitted matters to Imperial sanction, and coöperated united in mind and so guarded the Empire, we should undoubtedly be able to stand side by side with all the nations of of the world. I believe that there is nothing greater that Your Majesty's subject Yoshinobu can do in rendering service to the nation.[34]

This the Emperor Meiji accepted with pleasure. And on the ninth of December in the same year was issued the great command to restore the reins of government to the Throne. In this command one reads:

Now that the reins of government have been restored to the Throne and the foundation for recovering the nation's prestige has been laid, and since it has been learned that it is His Majesty's pleasure henceforth to abolish Regency, the seat of Chief Adviser to the Emperor, the Shogunate Government, etc.,—setting up for the present and provisionally the three posts of Prime Minister, Counselor, and Adviser,—and His

---

[33]There was another Tokugawa Yoshinobu with whom this fifteenth Tokugawa Shōgun, who governed A.D. 1866-1868, must not be confused. The *on* or Japanized Chinese reading for this latter Yoshinobu is Keiki, by which he is also known.

[34]The original is in *sōrōbun,* the old and difficult epistolary style, and is written almost entirely in Chinese characters, largely following Chinese syntax, a style which is quickly dying out and whose flavor is impossible to reproduce in a translation.

pleasure to take over the entire administration, and to share with all His subjects their joys and sorrows, in a way just and fair to all, by drawing no distinction between civil officials, military officers, courtiers, and others, by conforming in all things to the initial activities of the Emperor Jimmu [the first Emperor]; be it known that ye are to render service to the Emperor and the State by diligence and by cleansing yourselves of the traditional evil practices of extravagance and laziness.[35]

His Majesty thus gave encouragement so that the restoration, based on [the spirit of] the founding of the Empire by the Emperor Jimmu, should have for its objective the unification of the nation and the renovation of all State affairs, and that it should bring about the complete renewal of all administrative activities by a will to begin everything afresh. Again, in March [or, more accurately translated, the third month in the lunar calendar] in the first year of Meiji, His Majesty graciously issued the Charter Oath in Five Articles [A.D. 1868], and when we respectfully read what follows in the Imperial letter issued simultaneously, we witness His Majesty's august solicitude and firm determination to do honor to the divine spirits of the Imperial Ancestors and to spread abroad to all nations the glory of the State by taking the lead in facing hardships and adversities by taking the burden upon His Majesty's own gracious Person:

We desire, by taking an oath with all Government officials and lords of clans, to take over the august undertaking left Us by Our Ancestors, in Our Person to govern the entire realm so that Ye Our subjects may abide in peace, and that by and by the glory of the nation may spread far abroad across the seas and the whole realm may rest in the calm that pervades Mount Fuji's peak.

In this manner in the Meiji Restoration His Majesty abolished the evil practices of old and sought for knowledge over the whole world and at the same time exalted the great "god-handed" Way, making it a fundamental principle to follow the spirit that has from of old belonged to our nation.

---

[35]The passage is loosely constructed and is almost entirely composed of Chinese characters.

In this way there was carried out the retrocession of feuds by all the clans to the Emperor and further the abolition of clans and the introduction of prefectures; and thus the administration of the country was restored to the Imperial Household, bringing about the restoration of Imperial rule and the fulfillment of the great task of restoration. The awakening of the people with the Emperor as their center was herein manifested to the full. We certainly cannot afford to overlook the fact that the services rendered in lending a hand in this great enterprise and the meritorious deeds of the patriots deserve to be held in reverence, nor overlook how Yoshinobu, when faced with an offer by the French Minister to aid the feudal Government, absolutely declined this offer and put an end to everything in the way of foreign intervention.

In the written announcement to the Ancestral spirits issued on the eleventh of February, twenty-second year of Meiji [A.D. 1889], on the enactment of the Imperial House Law and the Constitution, the Emperor says:

We the Emperor with discretion and awe to the divine spirits of
The Imperial Ancestors
Do declare and say: We the Emperor, in keeping with the tremendous tasks coeval with Heaven and Earth, do succeed to the Imperial Throne and, holding firm unto the projects laid down of old, shall never fall. It is to be noted that because of the strides the course of events is taking and of the advances made in enlightenment, We have herein enacted the Imperial House Law and the Constitution, so that the injunctions bequeathed by
The Imperial Ancestors
May be made plain, that the Imperial House Law and the Constitution may be established, setting forth matters clearly in clauses and chapters, leaving a pattern for Our Offspring to follow and opening a Way for Our subjects to render assistance to the Throne, so that they may observe these Laws for ever and ever, to the end that the nation's foundations may be consolidated more than ever and the happiness of the people promoted.

And in the Imperial Rescript announcing the promulgation of the Constitution the Emperor says:

We count it Our true joy to see Our subjects prosperous and happy, and hence We proclaim this great immutable Law to Our subjects of this and future generations through the prerogative which We have received from Our Imperial Ancestors.

That is, in the Imperial House Law and the Constitution the Emperor for ever consolidated the very foundation of the Empire by graciously transmitting Laws in writing by appropriating to the progress of the times the cause of justice which was at the time of the founding of the nation as clear as the Sun and the stars. Our Constitution granted by the Emperor is a great, eternal, and immutable Law in which He says:

We make known that which Our Heir, Our subjects, and the descendants of Our subjects should observe for ever and ever.

And we see therein the firmness of the spirit of the founding of the Empire that runs through it all. Later, on October 30, 1890, His Majesty issued the Imperial Rescript on Education, and clearly pointed out how our national education finds its source in our national entity.

Thus we have seen that the unfolding of our history consists, in the case of the Emperor, in taking over and appropriating the injunctions bequeathed by the Imperial Ancestors and, in the case of his subjects, in "dying to self" in order to fulfill their duties and in loyally guarding and maintaining the prosperity of the Imperial Throne. Hence, this great spirit of union between high and low is a thing that has already been clearly shown in the founding of the Empire; and it is this great spirit that runs throughout history, which has shown forth its beauty from generation to generation even down to this day. Herein we witness the resplendent records of our history of which the Emperor has spoken in the Imperial Rescript of Boshin [forty-first year of Meiji, A.D. 1908] as being, "in their clearness like unto the Sun and the stars."

II

The Homeland and the Life of the People

Our homeland was, according to legend, brought to birth by the two highnesses, His Augustness Izanagi no Mikoto and her Augustness Izanami no Mikoto, and their relationship to us is that of fellow creatures. Our love for the homeland and her trees and grasses springs from such a sense of brotherly affection. In effect, our people's love for the homeland finds its source in the relationship of oneness that has come down from the divine ages, so that the homeland shares her life with the nation and, reared in the Way of our country, amply maintains all things, and, together with the people, serves the Emperor.

Thus the homeland is an essential in nurturing the life of the people, in maintaining and developing their livelihood, and in cultivating their spirit; and the intimate and profound relationship between the homeland, her natural features, and the people, amply manifests our national characteristics, and their traces are everywhere to be seen throughout our history.

Legends handed down from our distant ancestors were sifted and recorded, producing the *Kojiki,* and were compiled into the *Nihon-shoki,* as things that manifest our national character and clarify the very foundation of Imperial rule; and the [Empress *Gemmei's* or *Gemmyō's*] orders [A.D. 713] to select material for the *Fudoki* [Records of Natural Features] bespeak the deep-rooted relationship between our national entity and our homeland. Herein lie the strong ties that inseparably bind *Koji* (Ancient Matters) and *Fūdo* (Natural Features). In the legends of our nation is related the brotherhood of the homeland and the people. Our people's affection for the homeland and their inclination to become one with her is exceedingly strong, and this is shown by the manner in which those engaged in farming blend and conform to the changes of the seasons. These characteristics pervade the annual functions that surround their festivals and ceremonies and their very mode of life.

A "Poem composed by Kakinomoto no Asomi[1] Hitomaro [Kakinomoto no Hitomaro, died A.D. 729?] when he went up to the Temporary Palace of Yoshino," which appears in the *Mannyō-shū*, reads:

> Our Lord, "god-handed" and awe-inspiring, that ruleth in peace, builded a great palace by the River Yoshinu[2] that floweth full like a waterfall and, looking down on the Land hither and thither, beheld, as it were, in the overlapping ranges of Mount Aogaki the offerings of the mountain deity. In Spring adorning the scene with flowers and in Autumn with maple tints, the deity of the river that floweth alongside [?][3] the mountain, as if in preparation for the Emperor's table, setteth forth cormorant fishers in the upper parts of the stream and in the nether parts spreadeth fine fishing nets. O 'tis a divine reign wherein both mountains and rivers do serve the Lord!

> *Hanka*[4]
>
> Our "god-handed" Lord,
>   Whom mountains and rivers together serve,
> Launcheth forth in a boat on a stream
>   That floweth full.

Those who read this poem will be able to appreciate the mind of our people that looks on the homeland and her natural features. In short, both the people and the homeland serve the Emperor as one. It is with such a mind as this that the people feel affection for the homeland and her natural features, live in her midst, and engage

---

[1]The fortieth Emperor, Temmu, established eight classes among the court nobles of which the second in order is *Asomi*.

[2]Not Yoshino as elsewhere.

[3]The meaning of the original is not clear.

[4]A short thirty-one syllable *tanka* appended to a long *uta*.

themselves in industrial pursuits. This is due to the fact that in the divine ages the deities of heaven brought forth ourselves and our homeland as their fellow creatures.

THE LIFE OF THE PEOPLE

This mind of fellowship and union which makes possible the singleness of this national foundation constantly runs through our national life. Where this spirit is found, the life of the people at all times manifests itself not correlatively but singly.

In our country this spirit is seen in all periods and at all times, in spite of the vicissitudes in political and social institutions. In olden times the clans formed the basis of the national life and the unit of the economic life, and they comprised under the Emperor a body of people of one blood and of one mind. That is to say, people were all united into clans, with clan chiefs over communities of clansmen; and to these clans were affiliated a people unrelated to them by blood, with duties assigned to the clans and those affiliated to them; so that all sorts of people and things helped each other, comprising a State with the Emperor at their center. In this way in each clan the clan chief apotheosizes the clan deity, and the clansmen, too, unite with their clan chiefs in apotheosizing their ancestors. Thus through these religious rites the clan chiefs and the clansmen in perfect concord unite with their ancestors. It is in this that one sees the administrative activities, enlightenment, and occupations of the clans. In this manner the clan chiefs, leading these united bodies, rendered service to the Imperial Court.

These intimate, welded relationships constantly endured throughout history. These are things totally different from what we see in the egotistic, modern Western communities which lay emphasis on the ego, but, founded since the dawn of history on an uninterrupted spirit and facts which are one in essence, are manifestations of the lives of our people. One sees therein running through each family, each district, and the one nation, a spirit of amity and unity. In short, a characteristic of our national life lies in the merging into one, of people and people, and of people and things, under the Emperor. This is the reason for the existence of the Way in which the relationship between the Sovereign and his subjects should lie in righteousness, and in which the relationship between father and child should lie in feelings of attachment, and this is also why there runs through family life and national life a beautiful sentiment, with the Sovereign and his subjects united as one and with parents and their children living in concord.

OCCUPATIONS

The division of occupations among clans gave birth in time to a spirit of esteem for one's trade, and this in turn meant regard for one's family name, that is, one's own name. Names in ancient times in our country did not stand for names of individual persons but were the names of the occupations followed by [the various] clans. Here we witness our people's spirit of holding their occupations in honor and of highly esteeming their family name. And this regard for duties appears in Imperial edicts and many historical facts. In a term instituted by the Emperor Temmu [A.D. 673-686], too, for a court rank, one finds the use of the term, "Pursuance of One's Duties." This spirit of respect for work is the mind of *musubi*[5] seen in works of production, creation, and development; and is the basic spirit of our national industries. This spirit was of old best fostered in agriculture.

The name of our country, Toyoashihara no Mizuho no Kuni [Abundant Reed-plain Rice-ear Land], shows that agriculture, which formed the basis of the lives of the people in the dawn of our nation, was held in high esteem; and the fact that there are many fixed, annual festivals that have to do with agriculture is a manifestation of this spirit. We should perhaps draw serious attention to the fact that beginning with the Imperial Household and coming down to the people, deep veneration has been held by them in the enshrin-

---

[5]See section devoted to this subject in Book I Chap. IV.

ing of Amaterasu Ohmikami in the inner Shrine and of Toyouke Daijin [Great Deity Toyouke][6] in the outer Shrine.

Today, when commerce, industry, and such activities are, besides agriculture, being developed in their various spheres, as our people's occupations; the same august esteem which is shown in regard to agriculture is witnessed also in all these other industrial spheres. Her Majesty the Empress Meiji pointed out in a poem the importance due to commerce:

> Precious are the efforts among
> Traders that strive to outdo their own
> In making rich this Land of the Sun.

We should each, with a right understanding of this august spirit, follow his own occupation, keeping pace with the progress of the times.

---

[6]The goddess of cereals and daughter of His Augustness Izanagi and Her Augustness Izanami.

III

The Inherent Character of the People

NATURAL FEATURES AND INHERENT CHARACTER OF THE PEOPLE

Yamaga Sokō [A.D. 1622-1685][1] states in the *Chūchō Jijitsu:*

The Land of Japan stands high above the other nations of the world, and her people excel the peoples of the world.

And indeed her natural features are blessed with a temperate climate and beautiful mountains and rivers; and rich in vernal flowers and autumn tints and scenic changes that accompany the seasons, Japan (Oh-yashima no Kuni) has been referred to since her birth as a region adapted to the lives of the people and as a "Land of Peace." However, natural catastrophes that from time to time visit the nation in their utmost fury occasionally menace the lives of the people; but the people do not on this account fear nature, nor are they cowed before it. Disasters go rather toward tempering the people's spirits so as to make them indomitable and, by awakening in them a power to start afresh and by increasing their attachment for the homeland, strengthen more than ever their desire to become one with the Land. Clashes with nature such as are found in Western mythologies do not appear in our legends, and this homeland is to the Japanese a very paradise in which to live. It is not by mere chance that Yamato[2] has been written in Chinese characters, "Great Harmony."

A then modern, classical poem by Rai San-yō [A.D. 1780-1832], which has earned popular fame, reads:

A gaze across Yoshino's mount
Where the awakening glow of the cherry flowers ushers in
the dawn—
And the hearts of Chinese and Koreans that see
Must surely turn Yamato.

---

[1]Samurai of the Aizu Clan, a leading scholar of the Shushigaku, the official philosophy of the Tokugawa regime, and a noted military strategist.
[2]One of the very many names for Japan.

And this poem shows how our beautiful natural features have nurtured this heart of Yamato. Again, when we note, too, the words of a poem on the "Yamato Spirit of Japan" by Moto-ori Norinaga [A.D. 1730-1801],[3]

> What cherry blossoms are these
> That send forth their aroma in the morning sun!

we see how deeply Japanese sentiment is bound up with Japan's natural features. Furthermore, one reads in *Seiki no Uta*[4] by Fujita Tōko [A.D. 1806-1855]:[5]

> The sublime "spirit" of the universe
>   Gathers pure over this Land of the Gods—
> Rising high, it forms the Peak of Fuji;
>   Towering aloft, it kisses the skies to a thousand autumns—
> Pouring itself forth out of rivers, it flows as waters of
>   the great deep;
>   And boundless it courses around our Land—
> It blossoms forth as countless clusters of cherry flowers,
>   And nought there is compares to their clustered
>   beauty and scent.

And this sings of the manner in which our homeland, her trees and verdure vie to clothe our spirit and its beauty.

A CLEAN AND CLOUDLESS HEART

Such a homeland as this and the national life which centers round the family, and which is expressive of the concord between the sovereign and the people, have together brought forth our national character that is cloudless, pure, and honest. In effect, the following, which forms a part of an Imperial Rescript by the Emperor Mommu

---

[3] A renowned man of letters with fifty-five works, containing over a hundred and eighty volumes, to his credit.

[4] A poem of considerable fame, in the Chinese style, in praise of the sublimity of the universe.

[5] A patriot whose love of country was stamped with a hatred of foreigners.

[A.D. 697-707], on the occasion of his enthronement, is found repeated in this and in other passages:

> A genuine heart that is cloudless, pure, and candid;
> A candid heart that is pure, cloudless, and righteous.

This character also appears in our legends as the Shindō[6] spirit that
accompanies the purification rites; and in the name of an official
rank instituted by the Emperor Temmu [A.D. 673-686] in the fourteenth year of his reign the characters, "Cloudless," "Pure," and
"Honest," are placed above the rank name, "Pursuance of One's
Duties," showing how deeply this inherent national character was
esteemed. This translucence, purity, and honesty bespeak a spirit
of sterling quality, clothed in strength and candor, and this quality
is in short the utmost sincerity and truth. It is the actions and atti-
tudes, that stand for outward manifestations of this truth, that are
Pursuance of One's Duties. That is to say, the name of this official
rank was a manifestation of an open and fresh national character
and bespoke the people's attitude toward modes of life. Thus, a
cloudless, pure, and candid heart, whose intrinsic nature is truth,
does not confine itself merely to the world of sentiment; but as the
Emperor Meiji says in one of his poems:

> The valor of a Yamato heart
> When faced with a crisis
> Its mettle proves.

And this heart reveals itself as patriotism. It has been sung in the
Mannyōshū:

> Out to the deep,
> A watery corse—
> Across the hills,
> A grass-grown corse—
> Oh, I would die beside my Lord,
> Come what may![7]

---

[6]The Way of the Gods, and another name for Shinto.
[7]This passage is translated independently of the rendering of the same
Japanese text appearing in the second section, Book I, Chap. III.

And after the Mongolian Invasion the conception that this is the Land of the Gods developed notably, and was realized as the Yamato spirit. Indeed, the Yamato spirit has "prayed for the perpetuity and peace of the Imperial Throne," and in more recent times has been aroused forcibly and manifested concretely in the Sino-Japanese and Russo-Japanese Wars.

A pure, cloudless heart is a heart which, dying to one's ego and one's own ends, finds life in fundamentals and the true Way. That means, it is a heart that lives in the Way of unity between the Sovereign and his subjects, a Way that has come down to us ever since the founding of the Empire. It is herein that there springs up a frame of mind, unclouded and right, that bids farewell to unwholesome self-interest. The spirit that sacrifices self and seeks life at the very fountainhead of things manifests itself eventually as patriotism and as a heart that casts self aside in order to serve the State. On the contrary, a heart that is taken up with self and lays plans solely for self has been looked upon, from of old, as filthy and impure; so that efforts have been made to exorcise and to get rid of it. The purification ceremony as it exists in our country is a function in which one exorcises this adulterated heart and returns to the mainspring where the heart is pure, unclouded, and contrite. It is a function that has been practiced widely among our people ever since prehistoric times, and a passage in the Shinto purification rites reads:

Since thus informed, beginning with the Imperial Court of His Augustness the Imperial Grandchild and going on to all Lands under Heaven—that there might be nothing left that could be termed sin—exorcise and sanctify until no sin remains, we pray; as the God of Wind scattereth abroad the multifold clouds of Heaven; as the morning and evening winds do sweep aside the morning and evening mist; as the winds set free the bow of a large ship that lieth in a haven, and, setting free her stern, chaseth her free out to the great deep; as with a sharp, well-tempered sickle yonder shrubs are cut down to the roots. Then perhaps the Goddess Seoritsu Hime will bear our sins out to the great deep, a goddess whose abode is on the moving surface of the swift streams that tumble headlong from the heights of mountains lofty and low. If our sins are thus borne along, the Goddess Haya-akitsu Hime, whose dwelling is on the briny concourse of multitudinous sea streams of wild, briny tides, will surely swallow them up. If our sins are thus swallowed up, the God Ibukido-nushi that dwelleth at the door of spray spumes will surely spue them out into the nether land of the nether world. If our sins are thus spued out, the Goddess Hayasasura Hime, whose abode is in the nether land of the nether world, will surely carry them hence and bring them to nought. If our sins are thus brought to nought, from this day on and throughout the length and breadth of our realm there can be nothing left in the way of sin, beginning with the officials that serve at the Court of the Emperor . . .[8]

This passage indeed is an expression of the bright and sublime spirit of our purification ceremony. And our people have always preserved and exalted this pure, unclouded, and contrite heart by means of the purification rites.

When man makes self the center of his interests, the spirit of self-effacement and self-sacrifice suffers loss. In the world of individualism there naturally arises a mind that makes self the master and others servants and puts gain first and gives service a secondary place. Such things as individualism and liberalism, which are fundamental concepts of the nations of the West on which their national characteristics and lives are built, find their real differences when compared with our national concepts. Our nation has, since its founding, developed on the basis of a pure, unclouded, and contrite heart; and our language, customs, and habits all emanate from this source.

SELF-EFFACEMENT AND ASSIMILATION

In the inherent character of our people there is strongly mani-

---

[8]This Shinto prayer or address, whose opening and closing words are not given here, is rhetorically the finest of its kind. Its involved figures of speech, its play on words and names, its rambling style, and its mystical, poetic language, would suffer loss if the passage were rendered into the matter-of-fact English style of our day.

fested, alongside with this spirit of self-effacement and disinterestedness, a spirit of broadmindedness and its activities. In the importation of culture from the Asiatic Continent, too, in the process of "dying to self" and adopting the ideographs used in Chinese classics, this spirit of ours has coördinated and assimilated these same ideographs. To have brought forth a culture uniquely our own, in spite of the fact that a culture essentially different was imported, is due entirely to a mighty influence peculiar to our nation. This is a matter that must be taken into serious consideration in the adaptation of modern Occidental culture.

The spirit of self-effacement is not a mere denial of oneself, but means the living to the great, true self by denying one's small self. Individuals are essentially not beings isolated from the State, but each has his allotted share as forming parts of the State. And because they form parts, they constantly and intrinsically unite themselves with the State; and it is this that gives birth to the spirit of self-effacement. And at the same time, because they form parts, they lay importance on their own characteristics and through these characteristics render service to the State. These characteristics, in union with the spirit of self-effacement, give rise to a power to assimilate things alien to oneself. In speaking of self-effacement or self-sacrifice, one does not mean the denial of oneself toward the State, such as exists in foreign countries, where the State and individuals are viewed correlatively. Again, by broadmindedness and assimilation is not meant the robbery of things alien by depriving them of characteristics peculiar to them, thereby bringing about the loss of their individuality, but is meant the casting aside of their defects and making the best use of their merits; so that by searching widely one may enrich oneself. Herein do we find the great strength of our nation and the depth and breadth of our ideologies and civilization.

THE NATIONAL LANGUAGE

The spirit of self-effacement and unity clearly appears also in the national language. The Japanese language is characterized by the fact that the subject does not often appear on the surface, and also by its highly developed honorifics. This is due to the fact that things are not viewed from mutually opposite angles, but are weighed disinterestedly and as entireties. Thus, in foreign countries, whether in China or the West, honorifics are few; but in our country they have developed systematically since of old and are an eloquent manifestation of the spirit of respect; so that with the development of honorifics the use of the subject grew rare. This spirit of reverence, needless to say, means death to oneself with one's mind centered on the Imperial Household and for the sake of the Throne. This is seen in such examples as the use of *watakushi* ["private"] for the first person as against *ōyake* ["public"], and the turning of such verbs as *tamō, haberu,* or *saburō,* which have been in use from of old, into auxiliary verbs expressing respect or deference. Thus, from the term *saburō* or *samurō* [written *samurafu*] is derived the word *samurai,* which means a "knight"; and this accounts for the development of the epistolary style, *sōrōbun. Gozaimasu*[9] for instance, which is in use today, is composed of *goza-aru,* which stands for "honorable seat," and *masu,* which comes from *imasu,* meaning "is" or "is present."

MANNERS AND CUSTOMS

Next, in our manners and customs, too, we find a spirit of reverence for the deities and the Emperor, of self-effacement, and of concord. In referring to our daily meals, too, we speak of receiving our august meals,[10] and the practice of a whole household celebrating a meal after first placing the first fruits before the spirits of our ancestors by offering them to the deities goes to speak of the sentiment that food is received from the deities and that it is this same

---

[9] A polite affirmative ending.

[10] This is the literal meaning of a common expression, in which the verb "to receive" is an expression conveying an idea of receiving something from someone above you.

food of which we are partaking. In the New Year's functions, too, we see the traditional life that has come down to us from our distant ancestors in the planting of pine trees in front of our gates, in the use of water drawn for the first time in the year, and in the feast of the rice-cake soup. There is a connection between celebrating the New Year with the exchange of expressions of felicitation and the ancient spirit seen in the words of clan chiefs celebrating the Emperor's age.[11] The term *banzai*,[12] too, is a felicitous term having the same meaning.

Guardian deities, needless to say, and clan deities may be considered on the whole as deities of one's place of birth, and these have come down to us as forming the nuclei of the local life of communities. The Buddhist services performed during the equinoctial week and the Bon Festival of the Dead,[13] which are in practice today, are looked upon as a merging of Buddhist functions and the people's faith. Then again, in the Bon Festival dance seen in the precincts of tutelary shrines and temples one witnesses a merging and uniting of two streams of faith in the diversions of those living in farming villages. In the world of agriculture one witnesses such manifestations as the spirit of celebrating a good year for crops, of harmony and co-prosperity, and of ancestor worship; and again in our type of dance in which people form circles one sees a characteristic of self-effacement in uniting in a dance facing a center. And this is in contradiction to the types of dance in which men and women dance in couples, a feature common to Western community dances. There is a widely practiced custom of paying a visit to the local shrine when a child is born, and this is a manifestation of a sentiment toward the tutelary deity, which has come down to us from old times.

---

[11]People's ages are reckoned by the number of calendar years in which they have lived, so that every Japanese has a year added to his age on New Year's day; although the Western way of reckoning is also in use, the first being known as *kazoe* and the second as *man*.

[12]Literally, "ten thousand years"; but actually, "hurrah!"

[13]A Buddhist festival held on July fifteenth of the lunar calendar.

Among the annual functions are such things as the annual festivals, and in these are seen alliances to nature and the fusing and harmonizing of imported culture; and further, when we come to ancient court and military practices and usages, the traditional spirit that lies deep behind the outward forms of these activities cannot be overlooked. As already cited, among the annual functions there are those which carry traces of clan life, those which find their origin in Court life, and those which in the days of chivalry [A.D. 1192-1868][14] became established as ceremonial functions. At the root of all these functions one sees our glorious traditional spirit. In the Dolls' Festival the functions at first centered on exorcism; but with the ushering in of the life of the nobility in the Heian Period [A.D. 794-858] the thing turned into an amusement with dolls, and became a ceremonial function which combined in itself both pleasure and proper upbringing. Later on, with the arrival of the Edo [Yedo] Period [A.D. 1603-1868], the doll Emperor and Empress were placed in view, to foster the spirit of reverence for the Imperial Household.

---

[14]Referred to in Japanese history as Buke Jidai, when the government was in the hands of the military class.

I V

Ceremonial Rites and Morality

CEREMONIAL RITES

The Emperor Meiji was singing of the rites that ushered in our administrative activities at the beginning of the year when he wrote in one of his poems:

> This year again
> I would hear of the Ise Shrine
> Before all things.

In these rites the Prime Minister reports to the Throne the perfect manner in which ceremonial rites were conducted at the Shrine during the previous year. In this we see the great august Will to preside over ceremonial rites which are looked upon as of the greatest importance in the administrative activities of our nation. We read in the *Jingishi* in the *Dai Nihon-shi:*[1]

Ceremonial rites are the basis of religion and politics. If the entire realm vibrates with reverence for the deities, respect for one's ancestors, and devotion and honor toward one's parents, all systems and institutions will be established thereby.

And this brings out our national characteristics in which ceremonial rites, government, and education are united fundamentally. Our country is a divine country governed by an Emperor who is a deity incarnate. The Emperor becomes one in essence with the heavenly deities by offering them worship, and thereby makes all the more clear his virtue as a deity incarnate. Hence, the Emperor lays particular importance on ceremonial rites; and in the ceremonial rites

---

[1] A great history of Japan comprising 243 volumes, as already noted, completed in A.D. 1715. It did much toward raising the prestige of the Imperial dynasty and causing the Tokugawa to be regarded as usurpers. This compilation was resumed after the lifetime of Tokugawa Mitsukuni and finally completed in A.D. 1906 with a total of 397 volumes.

held in the three shrines in the Imperial Palace, namely, the Imperial Sanctuary, the Imperial Ancestors' Shrine, and the Imperial Tabernacle, the Emperor conducts the services himself. In the second year of Meiji [A.D. 1869], His Majesty sanctified and enshrined the deities of heaven and earth and the spirits of the successive Emperors by building a shrine within the Jingikan [in the grounds of the Bureau of Shinto Shrines], and in the third year [A.D. 1870], promulgated a Rescript consoling the spirits of the deities, saying:

We reverently call to mind how that Our Imperial Ancestor, at the time of the founding of the Empire, held the deities in high esteem, and loved and cared for the people. The genesis, therefore, of the unity of ceremonial rites and administration is seen to be in the very distant past. We, conscious of Our weakness, accede to the Throne; and day and night We are fearful lest We fall short in Our sacred mission. Wherefore, We now repose the spirits of the deities of heaven and earth, the spirits of the eight deities,[2] and the sacred spirits of the successive Emperors in the Jingikan [in the grounds of the Bureau of Shinto Shrines], and so give expression to Our devotion and reverence. We pray that Our subjects throughout the realm may follow this example.

It is the nature of the subjects to make this great august Will their own, to receive the spirit of the founding of the Empire as their own by means of ceremonial rites, to pray for the Emperor's peace by sacrificing themselves, and to enhance the spirit of service to the State. Thus, the Emperor's service to the deities and the subjects' reverence for the deities both spring from the name source; and the Emperor's virtues are heightened all the more by means of the ceremonial rites, and the subjects' determination to fulfill their duties is made all the more firm through their reverence for the deities.

Our shrines have served, from of old, as the center of the spirit of ceremonial rites and functions. Shrines are expressions of the great Way of the deities and places where one serves the deities and

[2]Namely: Kamimusubi no Kami, Takamimusubi no Kami, Tamatsu-memusubi no Kami, Ikumusubi no Kami, Tarumusubi no Kami, Ohmi-yanome no Kami, Miketsu Kami, and Kotoshironushi no Kami.

repays the source of all things and returns to their genesis. The Oracle on the Sacred Mirror is the object of the rites at the Shinto shrines and the Imperial Sanctuary;[3] and the fundamental significance of the existence of Shinto shrines is found in the Oracle on the Amatsu Himorogi [Heavenly Sanctuary] and the Amatsu Iwasaka [Sanctuary Precincts] in the passage on the descent to earth of the Imperial Grandchild, which appears in the *Nihon-shoki*. That is, this answers to the august Will expressed in the words of the deity Takamimusubi no Kami[4] addressed to their Augustnesses Ame no Koyane no Mikoto and Futotama no Mikoto:

We shall build the Amatsu Himorogi [Heavenly Sanctuary] and the Amatsu Iwasaka [Sanctuary Precincts] and offer services to the deities for the sake of Our Imperial Grandchild. Ye Augustnesses, Ame no Koyane no Mikoto and Futotama no Mikoto, descend Ye to Ashihara no Nakatsu Kuni,[5] bearing with You the Amatsu Himorogi, and offer Ye services also for the sake of Our Imperial Grandchild.

The deities enshrined in the Shinto shrines are the Imperial Ancestors, the ancestors of the clans descended from the heavenly deities or the Imperial Family,[6] and the divine spirits who served to guard and maintain the prosperity of the Imperial Throne. These ceremonial rites of the Shinto shrines serve to foster the life of our people and form the basis of this spirit. In the festivals of the clan deities one sees expressions of the spirit of repaying the source of all things and of returning to their genesis, and of the consequent concourse of clansmen. Then again, in the festival rites of the guardian deities, in which portable shrines are borne along, there is the friendly gathering of parishioners and the peaceful scenes of the

---

[3]Until B.C. 92 the Mirror was kept at the Imperial Palace; but the Emperor Sujin, awakening to the fact that it was too sacred a thing to be kept beside him since it reflected the very image of the Sun Goddess, Amaterasu Ohmikami, had a temple built for the Three Sacred Treasures.

[4]Spoken of in mythology as one of the three creators of the world.

[5]Literally, "Central Land of the Reed Plain," which is one of the many ancient names for Japan.

[6]Literally, "the Princes of the Ancestors of the Clans."

villages. Hence, Shinto shrines are also the center of the people's life in their home towns. Further, on national holidays the people put up the Rising Sun flag and unite in their national spirit of devotion to the State. Thus, all functions of the Shinto shrines ultimately unite in the services rendered by the Emperor to the Imperial Ancestors; and it is in this that we find the basis of our national reverence for the deities.

At festivals we serve the deities by purifying ourselves, with sincerity revere the dignity of the deities, return thanks for their benefits, and offer earnest prayers. The sentiment in coming before the deities springs in our country from the most fundamental element seen in the relationship between parents and children. In effect, it is found in drawing near to our ancestors by purifying ourselves of our sins and stains, in leaving self behind to unite with the public, and in "dying to self" to become one with the State.

And as a natural expression of a devout heart which has been purified we find an example in a poem by Saigyō Hōshi [A.D. 1118-1190][7] which reads:

> What is enshrined I do not know,
> But the awe of a sense of gratitude
> Brings tears to my eyes.

As Shinto shrines have their basic significance in being national existences, they have, since the establishment of the Bureau of Shinto Shrines in the Code of Laws,[8] come down to us as national organs and institutions; so that they are differently treated from all the Shinto sects[9] and other religions of a general nature.

A poem by the Emperor Meiji runs:

---

[7]He became a bonze at the age of twenty-three, abandoning his wife and children, and traveling through the provinces preaching and reciting poetry. This particular poem expresses his reaction as he came under the awe-inspiring influence of the Grand Shrine of Ise.

[8]Promulgated in the first year of the Taihō Era [A.D. 701].

[9]Of these there were thirteen.

> Great Goddess of Ise,
>> Preserve Our world,
> For which We pray,
>> "May this people
>> Rest well for aye."

Hafuribe Yukiuji also says in a poem:

> True is the heart
>> That serves my Lord
> When at the shrine it prays
> For a peaceful reign.

Thus, the Grand Shrine of Ise is the focal point of our Shinto shrines, and all shrines, as belonging to the State, form the pivot of the spiritual life of the people.

The true purport of our nation's ceremonial rites has been expounded in the foregoing passages; and when this is compared with faith toward God as it exists in the Occident, the result is a great gap. In the mythologies and legends of the West, too, mention is made of many deities; but these are not national deities that have been linked with the nation since the days of their origin, nor are they deities that have given birth to the people or the Land or have brought them up. Reverence toward deities in our country is a national faith based on the spirit of the founding of the Empire, and is not a faith toward a transcendental God in the world of Heaven, Paradise, Paramita [Sanskrit], or the ideal, but it is a spirit of service that flows out naturally from the historical life of the people. Hence, our ceremonial rites have a deep and broad significance, and at the same time are truly national and allied to actual life.

MORALITY

It is this spirit of reverence for the deities and one's ancestors that forms the basis of our national morality; and it is also this that has embraced and assimilated Confucianism, Buddhism, and other things imported from abroad into every field of our culture and created things truly Japanese. Our national morality is founded on reverence for the deities and our ancestors, and has brought forth the fruits of the great principle of loyalty and filial piety. By making the nation our home, loyalty becomes filial piety; and by making our homes our nation, filial piety becomes loyalty. Herein do loyalty and filial piety join in one and become the source of all good.

Loyalty means engaging ourselves zealously in our duties by making it our fundamental principle to be candid, clean, and honest, and it means fulfilling our duties, and thus to serve the Emperor; and by making loyalty our basic principle is filial piety established. This is the great Way of the deities which our people have faithfully followed since the days of their ancestors and throughout the past and the present.

In the Imperial Rescript on Education, His Majesty declared by way of teaching the fundamental principles of national morality:

Know Ye, Our Subjects: Our Imperial Ancestors have founded Our Empire on a basis broad and everlasting and have deeply and firmly implanted virtue; Our subjects, ever united in loyalty and filial piety, have from generation to generation illustrated the beauty thereof. This is the glory of the fundamental character of Our Empire, and herein also lies the source of Our education.

And he also says:

The Way here set forth is indeed the teaching bequeathed by Our Imperial Ancestors, to be observed alike by Their Descendants and the subjects, infallible for all ages and true in all places. It is Our wish to lay it to heart in all reverence, in common with you, Our subjects, that we may all thus attain to the same virtue.

That candor, purity, and honesty have been highly esteemed in our country is made evident by the fact that these appear in our legends, are seen in the Imperial edicts, and in the names of crowns according to rank. There is a passage in the *Hōkihongi*[10] which

---

[10]One of the sacred Shinto books [A.D. 725] which is reputed to be a forgery.

reads: "Honesty is the basis of divine protection." Again, in *Yamato-hime no Mikoto Seiki*[11] it says:

Behave with discretion and with utmost purity, with hearts made sincere, cleansed of sins. Move not to the right that which is on the left, nor move to the left that which is on the right; but serve the Great Goddess, keeping what is on the left on the left and what is on the right on the right, so that in returning to the left or taking a turn to the right ye may have nothing go amiss. This is because the genesis must be made the genesis and the source made the source.

This, in short, brings to light the spirit of candor, purity, and honesty, and it shows a heart which does not confuse the proper order of things, which speaks of things on the right as being on the right and of those on the left as being on the left, and which gives to all their proper place, making their respective duties clear and not going amiss in the least. And it is a heart that has no patience for anything crooked, and has no room for wickednesses and injustices. And it is only through this honesty that will not waver in the least and through its practice that we can make fundamentals our fundamentals. Kitabatake Chikafusa's [A.D. 1293-1354] *Jin-nōShōtōki* reflects this spirit and lays emphasis on honesty, and the name of the works attributed to him, namely, *Gengenshū*,[12] seems to have been taken directly from the foregoing passage; but what should be particularly borne in mind as national morality is to treat things on the left as being on the left and things on the right as being on the right, to have things abide in their true state and be as they should be, thereby making the genesis of things their genesis and the sources their sources.

BUSHIDŌ

Bushidō[13] may be cited as showing an outstanding characteristic

---

[11]A biography of Yamato Hime, the fourth Imperial Princess of the Emperor Suinin, traditionally the eleventh Emperor of Japan.

[12]Literally, "Source-Source-Collection."

[13]The Code of warriors; chivalry. Literally, "the way of warriors."

of our national morality. In the world of warriors one sees inherited the totalitarian structure and spirit of the ancient clans peculiar to our nation. Hence, though the teachings of Confucianism and Buddhism have been followed, these have been transcended. That is to say, though a sense of indebtedness[14] binds master and servant, this has developed into a spirit of self-effacement and of meeting death with a perfect calmness. In this, it was not that death was made light of so much as that man tempered himself to death and in a true sense regarded it with esteem. In effect, man tried to fulfill true life by way of death. This means that rather than lose the whole by being taken up with and setting up oneself, one puts self to death in order to give full play to the whole by fulfilling the whole. Life and death are basically one, and the monistic truth is found where life and death are transcended. Through this is life, and through this is death. However, to treat life and death as two opposites and to hate death and to seek life is to be taken up with one's own interests, and is a thing of which warriors are ashamed. To fulfill the Way of loyalty, counting life and death as one, is *Bushidō*.

In the Sengoku Period [A.D. 1490-1600],[15] too, the feudal lords gave ample expression to their patriarchal spirit and took good care of the serfs. This expression should also be true of *Bushidō*. The warrior's aim should be, in ordinary times, to foster a spirit of reverence for the deities and his own ancestors in keeping with his family tradition; to train himself to be ready to cope with emergencies at all times; to clothe himself with wisdom, benevolence, and valor; to understand the meaning of mercy; and to strive to be sensitive to the frailty of Nature. Yamaga Sokō [A.D. 1622-1685], Matsumiya Kanzan [A.D. 1686-1780], and Yoshida Shōin [A.D. 1831-1860] were all men of the devoutest character, who exercised much influence in bringing *Bushidō* to perfection. It is this same *Bushidō* that shed itself of the outdated feudalism at the time of

---

[14] The Japanese word expresses an idea strong and almost binding, for which there is no equivalent in English.

[15] The Age of Civil Wars.

the Meiji Restoration, increased in splendor, became the Way of
loyalty and patriotism, and has evolved before us as the spirit of the
Imperial Forces.

BUDDHISM

Buddhism was cradled in India, and was introduced into our
country by way of China and Korea. It is a faith as well as a rule
of morals, and at the same time a system of knowledge. Hence, its
introduction into our country saw its fusion into and sublimation
in our national spirit; and it developed in a way befitting the people.
Far back in history, in the "vernal" February in the reign of the
Empress Suiko [A.D. 593-628], it pleased Her Majesty to issue an
Imperial edict to devote more attention toward the elevation of the
Sampō;[16] and through this edict temples and pagodas were built to
answer to Imperial benevolences and parental attentions. This traditional spirit of the early days of Buddhism, to build temples in
answer to Imperial and parental benevolences, manifested itself later
as the spirit of national defence in Nanto Buddhism;[17] and this was
made the dictum by the Tendai[18] and Shingon[19] Sects. This spirit
later on took shape in the advocacy for protecting the nation by
reviving the teachings of Zen in the case of the Rinzai Sect,[20] and

---

[16]Literally, "the Three Treasures" (*Ratnatraya*); namely, the Buddha
(Perfect Person), Dharma (Truth), and Sangha (Community). But it has
come to connote Buddhism.

[17]The older sects of Buddhism, mainly Hīnayāna, belonging to the Nara
Period; Nanto meaning, Southern Capital, namely, Nara.

[18]Saichō, later known as Dengyō Daishi, was sent to study Buddhism in
China in the year A.D. 802. He studied a form of Buddhism which had its
headquarters at Mount T'ien-t'ai, and upon his return to Japan in A.D. 805
introduced it as the Tendai Sect of Japan with headquarters at Mount Hiei,
near Kyōto.

[19]Kūkai, more popularly known as Kōbō Daishi, went to China in A.D.
804, where he studied the esoteric teachings of the Chên-yen (Shingon) Sect
of China under Hui-Kuo. He returned to Japan and introduced his version of
the esoteric Buddhist teachings in A.D. 807 through the Shingon Sect which
he founded.

[20]A branch of the Zen Sect.

in the advocacy for assuring the peace of the State by the rule of righteousness in the case of the Nichiren Sect. Besides, the founders of new Buddhist sects similarly esteemed the laws established by the Throne. Hence, their doctrinal developments, too, were truly noteworthy. The spirit of reverence for the deities of heaven and earth and of unity and self-effacement that centers on Amaterasu Ohmikami is found in the teaching of the Shingon Sect, which holds that everything in the universe is a manifestation of *Mahavairocanasatathagata* and that each mind is a living Buddha, and in the teaching of the Tendai Sect, which declares that there is Buddhahood in plants and trees as well as the homeland, saying that even a *Bala*[21] is a Buddha when enlightened and that the whole creation has access to *vimockcha*.[22] And one also finds in these things the spirit of universal benevolence and something that accords with a mind that embraces all. Some of the sects of Nanto Buddhism preach discrimination in *vimockcha;* but after the days of Heian Buddhism equality of all came to be preached, with clarification of the original purport of Buddhism which, based on self-annihilation, stood in particular for the idea of equality in spite of individual differences and of differences in spite of the fact that all are equal. This is due to the fact that their doctrines were likewise adapted and sublimated through our clan and family spirit and our self-effacing and totalitarian spirit, which our nation possesses as believing in equality in spite of individual differences. For instance, we see Shinran [A.D. 1173-1262][23] speaking of his fellow men as comrades and as companions on the way. The Jōdo and Shin Sects held the tenets of salvation by faith by means of Buddhist invocations as against the tenets of salvation by works, and so preached the instability of life, while

[21] A common man; a mortal; a sinner (Sanskrit).
[22] Deliverance; salvation (Sanskrit).
[23] A famous bonze and founder of the Shin Sect. Was early taught the doctrines of the Tendai Sect, and was later taught the doctrines of the Jōdo Sect by Hōnen (same as Genkū), whom he followed. Satisfied with neither sect, he formed a new sect, the Jōdoshin Sect, which means, the true sect of Jōdo.

the Ji Sect went on pilgrimages in order to indoctrinate and trans-
form others; and in this manner these sects made Buddhism a
religion of the masses. In Shinran's search after natural law by
preaching absolute belief in salvation by faith in Amida Buddha,
fullest play is given to the spirit of self-effacement and unity; while
the manner in which teachings carried on by Hōnen [A.D. 1133-
1212][24] by chanting prayers irrespective of time or place to the
effect that one should fulfill the "mission" of death in one's natural
state portrays the kinetic and practical view of life taken by the
Japanese. Again, there is a similarity in the disinterested and practical stand taken by Dōgen [A.D. 1200-1253], who looked on industries and measures to control natural havoc as works done in
return for benefits received, believing that deeds done by those who
have emptied themselves of self indeed comprised the Way. This
spirit gradually took form in a view, for instance, that the three
religions, Shintoism, Confucianism, and Buddhism, harmonized
with each other. One sees a spirit of esteem for history and tradition
in the rise of the movement for return to Shōtoku Taishi [A.D. 572-
621],[25] in the Tendai and other sects, which made as their basis the
teachings of masters historically transmitted from generation to
generation from Sakya[26] down. In this manner, our nation, which
has been looked upon as adapted to Mahāyāna Buddhism, has made
Buddhism what it is today; and in this we see naturally manifested
a true picture and character of the people befitting the nation. It is
Buddhism assimilated in this manner that has enriched our culture,
deepened our way of looking at things, schooled us in meditation,
and permeated our national life, at the same time inciting our

[24]See preceding note. He propagated the doctrines of the Jōdo Sect with
great success, and professed that salvation or entrance into the "pure land,"
Jōdo, can be obtained only by prayer, setting an example by repeating the
name of Amida as often as sixty thousand times a day.

[25]One of the most important figures in Japanese history and Buddhism. He
was, furthermore, the first one to send an embassy to China (A.D. 607), and
it is to him that Japan owes the adoption of the Chinese calendar (A.D. 604).

[26]Or, Gautama.

national spirit, and giving rise to functions in which reverence for one's ancestors is seen, as in the case of Paramita and Ullambana [Sanskrit].

V

National Culture

CULTURE

Our culture is a manifestation of the great spirit that has come down to us since the founding of the Empire. In order to enrich and develop this, foreign culture has been assimilated and sublimated. In the *Gozatsuso,* a product of the Ming Dynasty in China, there is a tradition, in that part forming Chinese classics bearing on the teachings of the sages, which says that if there should be anyone going over to Japan carrying with him the works of Mencius his boat would be overturned and those on board be drowned. This goes to show that all revolutionary ideas are basically contrary to our national entity and proves the existence of our resolute spirit and our impartial judgment which is based thereon. It was in this sense, too, that the expression, "The combining of the Japanese spirit and Chinese literary talent," which is attributed to Sugawara no Michizane [A.D. 845-903], was in popular use.

No true culture should be the fruit of abstract individual ideas alienated from the State and the race. Every cultural feature in our country is an embodiment of our national entity. When one looks upon culture as developments of abstract ideas, the result is always separation from concrete history, and the inevitable is something abstract and universal that transcends national boundaries. However, in our culture there always subsists the spirit of the founding of the Empire, and this spirit is one in essence with our history.

Thus, our national culture is consistent in spirit and at the same time brings to view characteristics differing with every stage of history. Hence, creation always means union with retrospection, and restorations always become the generative power behind reformations. That means that the present and the past unite in one; and it is here that creative activities of a new era are carried on. Those tracing the history of our nation will doubtless see this fact clearly manifested on every page. Hence, in our country creative activities that ignore acts of restoration are not creative activities in the true sense of the term. At the same time, acts of restoration without creative activities are not true acts of restoration. Only in *musubi*,[1] which is based on the spirit that has come down to us from the founding of the Empire, must we find the true picture of the development of our nation.

SCHOLASTIC PURSUITS

Scholastic pursuits in our country have from the beginning progressed through the august patronage of the successive Emperors, and it is to their patronage that we owe the advancement which we see today. That is to say, the Emperors adopted, from of old, Confucianism and Buddhism as well as the allied cultures of the Continent, giving them due attention and patronage. We should have no time to enumerate what the Emperors have done, had we to start mentioning how they widely adopted the quintessence of foreign cultures by despatching envoys to the Sui and T'ang Dynasties together with numerous students and priests to study abroad, or of how they gave encouragement to scholastic pursuits by effecting the compilation by Imperial command of the *Kokin Wakashū*[2] and of works that followed down to and including what is generally known as the *Nijūichidai-shū*,[3] following the compilation of the *Mannyōshū*, not to mention the publication of works through Imperial command. This Imperial patronage is witnessed in more recent times since the Meiji Restoration in the Emperor Meiji's solicitude toward the assimilation and propagation of Occidental learning and technique. Thus, it is solely because of the great august desire to disseminate the august spirit of the founding of the Empire

---

[1] See section entitled, *Musubi* and Harmony, in Book I, Chapter IV.

[2] Or, *Kokinshū* (literally, "A Collection of Ancient and Modern Poems"). The work forms twenty volumes comprising over 1,100 poems, mainly *tanka*.

[3] Twenty-one collections of poems, from the *Kokinshū* (A.D. 905) to the *Shinzoku Kokin Wakashū* (fifteenth century).

by the Imperial Ancestor and to bring about the prosperity of the nation and to further the well-being of the subjects that the Emperor gave scholastic pursuits due attention and patronage.

From ancient times and since the founding of the Empire a consistent spirit has run through this nation's scholastic pursuits. Shōtoku Taishi adopted the teachings of Confucius, Buddha, and Lâo-tzŭ to further the Imperial Way, and built up a Code of Laws in Seventeen Chapters, and also produced the *Sangyō no Gisho*.[4] In expounding "reason," namely, "the logic of things," it was by no means an abstract, universal law that he was referring to, but he was setting forth "reason" as a Way based on the traditional spirit that is consistently practical. Thus, by means of this Way forms of knowledge and culture covering many fields were synthesized and unified, and ever since then works of creation and restoration, as well as tradition and advancement, have developed hand in hand, bearing fruits of progress.

In the field of history, Shōtoku Taishi early produced the *Tennōki*[5] and the *Kokki*;[6] while the Empress Gemmei [Gemmyō A.D. 708-714], following the Will of the Emperor Temmu [A.D. 673-686], had the three volumes of the *Kojiki* compiled; and the Empress Genshō [A.D. 715-723], by issuing an Imperial order, brought about the compilation of the thirty volumes of the *Nihon-shoki*. And from the year following the choice place given to the *Nihon-shoki*, Her Majesty set up a lectureship within the Imperial Palace and caused her subjects to discern clearly the true form of the nation. The work of compiling historical material by Imperial order was continued down to the reign of the Emperor Go-Daigo [A.D. 1319-1338], and saw the completion of the *Rikkokushi*,[7] witnessing the undertaking by civilians of a later generation of a work of compiling historical material such as the *Dai Nihon-shi*. Again, the study of things

---

[4]The first commentary on the Buddhist scriptures by the Japanese.
[5]A collection of the biographies of various Emperors.
[6]A historical work known to have existed but now lost.
[7]Six major historical works on Japan.

Japanese that sprang up in the Edo Period is a renaissance of learning based on the study of the classics, and it greatly contributed, together with history, toward elucidating the significance of our national entity and toward enhancing our national spirit.

Our scholastic pursuits one and all find their culmination in our national entity and see their mission in guarding and maintaining the prosperity of the Imperial Throne. The carrying out of researches in the face of tremendous difficulties when the Edo Period saw the introduction into our country of such sciences as medicine and ballistics, and the assiduous application and efforts made in the adoption of many Occidental sciences following the Meiji Restoration, were things made possible by keeping to the Way of the subjects whose principle is to guard and maintain the prosperity of the Imperial Throne. Nevertheless, in the scholastic pursuits of our day in which foreign cultures are being imported at a tremendous pace and great advancements made in every field, we cannot say for certain that there is no danger of unconsciously losing sight of this focal point. The Emperor Meiji says in the Charter Oath in Five Articles:

Seek knowledge throughout the world and greatly add to the life of the foundation of the Imperial regime.

Hence, those engaged in scholastic pursuits, whatever the field, must have their minds concentrated on this fundamental object and not deviate from the principal aim of our nation's scholastic pursuits, and thus strive to comply with the Imperial Will.

EDUCATION

That education in our country is also wholly based on our national entity, that it makes the manifestation of this national entity its focal point, and that it has its distant source in the Way handed down to us since the founding of the Empire, is a fact we have seen to be equally true in the case of scholastic pursuits. In the old days, when clan chiefs rendered services at the Imperial Court,

taking their parishioners with them, education consisted in the
handing down of the history of services rendered by their ancestors.
For example, we see in the genealogy of the Takahashi family how
they gave injunctions to their posterity and thereby instilled fervor
into their sense of duty by relating step by step how their ancestor,
Iwakamutsukari no Mikoto, excelled in loyal service to the Emperor Keikō [A.D. 71-130], and how subsequently generation after
generation carried on the family vocation and served as Imperial
Household officials in the Imperial Court. Genealogies that have
followed are all of this type. In the education of the knights in later
generations, too, importance was laid on family education according
to this tradition, and instructions were always given to preserve the
family name. What appears in the written pledge of Kikuchi Takemochi, which forms the family precepts of Kikuchi, a loyal subject
of the Yoshino Court, is a good example:

Since I, Takemochi, born of a family of knights, do render service at
the Imperial Court, do pray that the Three Treasures[8] may see my way
to establishing myself in the world through the benevolence of the Imperial Court, I myself doing honor to my family name by following the
laws of honesty in compliance with the Way of Heaven. I hope, besides,
never to be a knight that forgets righteousness or makes light of shame
through his own ambitions or greed with a heart taken up with the affairs of the world.

Education in recent times has owed much to the activities of the
Shintoists, scholars of Japanese classics, Confucianists, Buddhist
scholars, moral philosophers. Among these activities reverence for
the Purification Ceremony of Nakatomi[9] among the Shintoists or
the studies and dissemination of our classics among scholars of
Japanese classics are the most noteworthy. Hand in hand with contributions by these people go the reading aloud of poems before

---

[8]Namely, Buddhism.
[9]The grand purification ceremonies held on the last day of June and of
December.

the deities at the shrines and the offering of tablets, even including votive tablets that have to do with computations. The rise of the various pursuits is traced to the deities; for instance, in the setting up of guardian deities as founders of various artistic pursuits, the revering of the Hachiman Shrine as enshrining a military deity, the looking up to Temman Tenjin[10] as a man of letters, and in tracing of the origin of the *waka*[11] to the sacred poem of *Yakumo* by His Augustness Susano-o no Mikoto.

Just as the word *oshi*[12] signifies "to love," *oshie* (to teach) means "to rear tenderly"; and it means the rearing of mankind in compliance with the Way on the basis of man's natural affection. "To guide" means the guiding of your children so that they may reach the Way. Just as the Emperor Meiji enjoined in the Imperial Rescript on Education, our education, for one thing, comprises the spirit of guarding and maintaining the prosperity of the Imperial Throne by following the august spirit manifested in the founding of the Empire in keeping with our national entity. Hence, this is entirely different in its essence from the mere development and perfection of oneself such as is seen in the idea of self-realization and perfection of one's character as set forth in individualistic pedagogics. In short, it is not a mere development of individual minds and faculties set apart from the nation, but a rearing of a people manifesting the Way of our nation. Education whose object is the cultivation of the creative faculties of individuals or the development of individual characteristics is liable to be biased toward individuals and to be led by individual inclinations, and in the long run to fall into an unplanned education, and so to run counter to the principles of the education of our country.

Education must be such that it treats knowledge and practice as one. Education that lays one-sided emphasis on knowledge and lacks in practical application by the people is in contradiction to the

---

[10]Names under which Sugawara no Michizane (A.D. 845-903) is honored.
[11]A Japanese poem of thirty-one syllables.
[12]The Chinese character with this *kana* reading is "love."

true aim of our nation's education. That is, it is to be noted that the true object of our national education is seen in walking the Way of the founding of our Empire with knowledge and practice united in one. All systems of knowledge take shape only through practice and in this manner fulfill their object; and at the base of inductive knowledge there should always be a deep conviction that is linked with our national entity and practice related thereto. Hence, national conviction or application gains in accuracy and develops more and more through inductive knowledge; so that in our education, too, inductive or scientific knowledge must be given attention and encouragement. And this knowledge must, at the same time, contribute to the true advancement of our national civilization by keeping it under the influence of national conviction and practice. In other words, we should devote our efforts on the one hand toward the development of the various fields of the numerous sciences and on the other take heed to their synthesis, elevate them into practice, and thereby fulfill the aims of these spheres of knowledge, giving expression to their special features.

The Emperor Meiji graciously said in 1879 in the Outline of Education and Studies:

It is the teaching of Our Ancestors, the spirit of our national laws, and what is looked upon by the entire nation as a model of teaching, to count as most vital in education and studies the following of the Way of mankind by clarifying the Way of humanity and justice and of loyalty and filial piety, by exhausting the resources of knowledge and of talent, and accomplishments.

Howbeit, there have of late been not a few who have given weight solely to knowledge, talent, and accomplishments, not fathoming the real purport of civilization and enlightenment, breaking the laws of ethics and corrupting public morals. This is to be accounted for by the fact that toward the early part of the Meiji Restoration the good points of Western countries were at one time assimilated and daily progress made with the excellent idea of breaking away in the main from old abuses and of adopting knowledge from all over the world. Nevertheless, it is feared that if, as an unfortunate result, foreign ways are copied without due thought—with ideas of humanity, righteousness, loyalty, and filial piety set aside—the great principle binding the Sovereign and his subjects, and the fathers and their children, will in course of time be forgotten. This would not be in keeping with the primary purpose of our education and studies.

This behooves us indeed to reflect on matters deeply, with the present times viewed in the light of these factors.

ARTISTIC PURSUITS

Our national Way stands out markedly in the arts that have come down to us from of old. Poetry, music, calligraphy, painting, the incense cult, the tea ceremony, flower arrangement, architecture, sculpture, industrial arts, and dramas, all culminate in the Way, and find their source therein. The Way manifests itself on the one hand as a spirit of esteem for tradition and on the other as creative or progressive activities. Thus, our artistic pursuits, ever since the Middle Ages, have been practiced by first keeping to the norms, and by later laying emphasis on cultural methods of getting away from these norms. This means that they taught that artistic pursuits should be materialized along one's personality only after one has personally found the Way by casting aside one's untoward desires and by first following the norms in keeping with tradition. This is characteristic of our artistic pursuits and training therein.

One of the basic characteristics of our artistic pursuits is the adoption of modes based on the spirit of disinterestedness and the existence of an attitude to conform still further with nature. In building gardens, too, what is sought for is a blending with the natural scenery forming the background, the enjoyment of a replica of a natural landscape through a happy distribution of every tree and stone, and a sheltering in the bosom of Mother Nature by putting up a bower of bamboo frames and a thatched roof. In short, this characteristic is not of a nature that gives way to subjective plans or pampers public sentiment. The high place given to chaste refinement,[13] too, is a result of a demand that through this means the Way be conformed to by forgetting oneself. The object is to enjoy squatting face to face in a narrow tearoom as if to meet for once in one's lifetime, and to enter into the flavor of a merging of personalities among master and guests, and so to arrive at a state of concord in a gathering of all classes of people with self set aside and with no idea of discrimination. This spirit corresponds with the way in which people of different classes and occupations have from of old cultivated a great spirit of selfless service through concord as between equals in spite of differences. In the field of painting, too, the Yamatoe paintings are guileless presentations of people and nature; are elegant and most tasteful, and are finest representations of the Japanese mind. The *renga*[14] and the *haikai*[15] are originally not individual compositions, but literature produced by groups of people, in harmony and through coöperation. Again, the chaste and unsullied architecture of shrines harmonizes beautifully with nature and is endlessly serene and awe-inspiring. These characteristics appear widely in the fine and industrial arts as well; as witness, for instance, the temples that merge gracefully with the surrounding mountains, rivers, and verdure, or the concurrence with nature seen even in such things as designs on armor, helmets, and clothing. Another feature to be noted as regards our national arts is the composite harmony between the spiritual and the actual and the union of their different fields. For example, this deep relationship of oneness between mind and matter is ably presented in Seami's [A.D. 1363-1443] "Flowers," Bashō's [A.D. 1644-1694] "Sabi,"[16] and

[13]The word translated "chaste refinement" is *wabi*, whose meaning would be better understood by the Japanese by *shibumi*, for which there is no English equivalent. It represents an artistic quality which is the very opposite of the flowery.

[14]The *waka* composed by two people, in which the first is generally done by one person and the second half by another.

[15]The same as *hokku*.

[16]A certain characteristic sentiment peculiar to Japanese art which comprises loneliness and resignation, a word for which there is no English equivalent.

Chikamatsu Monzaemon's [A.D. 1653-1724] "On Truth and False-hood." In picture scrolls one finds the masterly syntheses of literary, pictorial, and industrial arts, etc.; and in the *Nō* dance there is a vivid, synthetic manifestation of verses and songs, instrumental accompaniments, dances, and performances, pictorial and industrial arts, etc. In the *Kabuki,* too, characteristics of the play are seen in the happy fusion of its music, dancing, and gestures; and its charac-teristics extend to the concord between the stage and the audience by means of a long outer passage leading to the stage.

In a word, our culture is in its essence a manifestation of the great spirit of the founding of the Empire; and scholastic pursuits, education, artistic pursuits, etc., all spring from one and the same source. Our future national culture, too, must be increasingly evolved in keeping with a Way such as this.

VI

Political, Economic, and Military Affairs

UNITY OF RELIGIOUS RITES AND THE STATE

In our country religious rites and the administration spring from the same source, under the august rule of the Emperors who succeed each other in an unbroken line. When adopting the institutions of the T'ang Dynasty at the time of the Taika Reform, the Emperor Kōtoku [A.D. 645-654] asked how to rule his subjects happily, whereupon Soga no Ishikawamaro respectfully replied,

> First enshrine the deities of heaven and earth, and that done one shall devote his attention to affairs of government.

Our ancient written law was completed over a period extending from the institution of the Ohmi Codes[1] to that of the Yōrō Codes;[2] and the early part of the Law relating to Government Officials provides that shrine administrators should be set up, and in particular it has a Law relating to Shrines [Jingirei, or Jingiryō]. The Emperor Meiji declares by way of an edict:

> To revere the deities of heaven and earth and to lay importance on ceremonial rites is the Code of the Empire and the basis of religion and the State.

This means that since the founding of the Empire the spirit of ceremonial rites has been the basis of administrative affairs; and in the Imperial Palace His Majesty graciously administers the ceremonial rites of the three Sanctuaries with the utmost dignity. We are reverently informed that this is an expression of His Majesty's partaking of the august spirit of the founding of the Empire by the Imperial Ancestor and of the great august mind to rule over his people during his reign in the Way handed down by the deities.

---

[1] Law code drafted in the second half of the seventh century.
[2] The Ohmi Codes as revised by the Empress Genshō in A.D. 718.

Truly, reverence for the deities and love for their subjects are the great august Will of the successive Emperors.

CONSTITUTION GRANTED BY THE EMPEROR

The Emperor Meiji, transmitting the teachings bequeathed by the Imperial Ancestors and the great law marking the reigns of the successive Emperors, graciously enacted the Imperial House Law on February 11, 1889, and promulgated the Constitution of the Japanese Empire.

The written Constitutions of foreign countries have come into existence as a result, in the main, of expelling or suppressing the existing ruler. In the case of a Constitution resulting from the expulsion of a ruler, the thing is called a Constitution Based on Social Contract; but in reality it is not a thing contracted by a people on an equal level and on a free footing, but is nothing short of a thing settled upon by winners in a struggle for power. A Constitution resulting through the suppression of a ruler is referred to as a Constitution Contracted between Ruler and People; and this is nothing but a matter agreed upon between a ruler traditionally in power and a rising influence which coerces him to enter into an agreement touching their respective spheres of influence. Moreover, there may be other Constitutions styled, Constitution Granted by the Throne; but the difference is only a matter of degree, so that in essence they are nothing short of the type of constitution based on contract.

However, our Imperial Constitution is a Constitution Granted by the Throne which the Emperor who comes of a line unbroken for ages eternal has instituted in perfect accord with his great august Will by virtue of the "supreme authority bestowed upon him by the Imperial Ancestors;" so that, together with the Imperial House Law, it is indeed nothing short of an Imperial edict.

Hence, the substance of this Constitution granted by the Throne is not a thing that has been turned into a norm, in order to stabilize for ever, as in foreign countries, the authoritative factors to the time of the enactment of a Constitution. Nor is it the fruit of a systematization of abstract ideas or practical requirements of such things as democracy, government by the law, constitutionalism, communism, or dictatorship. Nor again is it an imitation or adaptation of a foreign system, but it is nothing less than the great law of administration clearly manifested in the injunctions bequeathed by the Imperial Ancestors. This is made clear by what His Majesty declares in his august message addressed to the divine spirits of the Imperial Ancestors, when about to grant the Imperial House Law and the Constitution, whose burden is that

the injunctions bequeathed by
The Imperial Ancestors
May be made plain, that the Imperial House Law and the Constitution may be established, setting forth matters clearly in clauses and chapters;

and whose purport is that the enactment

is merely a transmission of the great law of government bequeathed by the Offspring of
The Imperial Ancestors.

That this great august Will to transmit the august teachings of the Imperial Ancestors remained unchanged throughout the entire reign of the Emperor Meiji, including, needless to say, the occasion of the enactment of the Imperial House Law and the Constitution of the Japanese Empire, is borne witness to by His Majesty's august poems which read:

Whatever progress the world may see,
Pray, let us abide by the law of our Land,
Which is of yore.

Nought but the thought that We may not break
The laws of the age of the gods—
Is Our prayer sincere.

The laws of our Land that we have made
Were the voices, mark! of the honored Lords
That breathed of yore.

And what is more, such an august Will is not confined to the reign of the Emperor Meiji, but runs through the reigns of all the Emperors. The august teachings bequeathed by the Imperial Ancestors are transmitted by the successive Emperors, and it is herein that one sees the blessed truth that the unbroken line of Emperors is not only a natural unbroken line, but that it is at the same time an unbroken line of which the Emperor is augustly conscious. Hence, we must accept the Imperial House Law and the Constitution of the Japanese Empire as transmissions of the great law of government bequeathed by the Imperial Ancestors to their descendants, and humbly interpret them with awe and put them into practice.

And this transmission of the great law of continuous august government in the fresh form of the Imperial House Law and the Constitution of the Japanese Empire appears in the august address to the spirits of the deities, namely:

It is to be noted that because of the strides the course of events is taking and of the advances made in enlightenment, We have herein enacted the Imperial House Law and the Constitution, so that the injunctions bequeathed by

The Imperial Ancestors

May be made plain, that the Imperial House Law and the Constitution may be established, setting forth matters clearly in clauses and chapters, leaving a pattern for Our Offspring to follow and opening a Way for the subjects to render assistance to the Throne, so that they may observe these Laws for ever and ever, to the end that the nation's foundations may be consolidated more firmly than ever and the happiness of the people promoted.

The Emperor's prayer for the prosperity of the nation, the enhancement of his subjects' virtues and talents, and for the promotion of their happiness, is accounted for by the fact that he conforms to "the great undertakings coeval with heaven and earth" and "stabilizes for ever the tasks left him by the Imperial Ancestors." Hence, we respectfully note that the Emperor's object in granting the Constitution lies in setting forth clearly a criterion to which both Sovereign and subject should conform, and in making widely known a Way by which the subjects may render assistance to the Throne. Hence, the progress of the times and the advancement of civilization have served as opportunities for the august enactment of the Constitution. And in this, too, the Emperor is seen as following the injunctions of an Imperial Ancestor which says:

When a sage establishes laws, his principles are always made to comply with the trend of the times.

When we note the august spirit to establish a Constitution, such as referred to, and turn our attention to the origins of the enactment of Constitutions among foreign nations, we can understand the essential differences between our Constitution and those of foreign nations.

Among the injunctions bequeathed by the Imperial Ancestors that are carried over into our Constitution the most thoroughly basic is the Oracle which is coeval with heaven and earth. This Oracle is the great august Will of the line of Emperors unbroken for ages eternal, is at the same time the prayer of the myriad gods and goddesses and of the entire nation. Hence, whether we are conscious of the fact or not, it is an imperative that actually exists and acts as a law. It is not merely a pattern that serves as a guide for the future, but is a great reality that has come down to us since the founding of the Empire. Article I of the Constitution which reads,

The Empire of Japan shall be reigned over and governed by a line of Emperors unbroken for ages eternal,

serves to set forth this fact. Article II sets forth the qualifications and precedence for succession to the Imperial Throne; while the first half of Article IV serves to carry the purport of Article I a step further by means of new ways of thinking assimilated since the Meiji Restoration in regard to such matters as sovereignty and administrative rights. The Emperor is the holder in essence of supreme power; so that the theory which holds the view that sovereignty lies in essence in the State and that the Emperor is but its organ has no foundation except for the fact that it is a result of blindly following the theories of Western States. The Emperor is not merely a so-called sovereign, monarch, ruler, or administrator, such as is seen among foreign nations, but reigns over this country as a deity incarnate in keeping with the great principle that has come down to us since the founding of the Empire; and the wording of Article III which reads, "The Emperor is sacred and inviolable," clearly sets forth this truth. Similar provisions which one sees among foreign nations are certainly not founded on such deep truths, and are merely things that serve to ensure the position of a sovereign by means of legislation.

DIRECT RULE BY THE EMPEROR

Furthermore, the other provisions of the Imperial Constitution are standing rules for government by the Emperor who possesses all these essential qualities. Above all, the basic principles underlying the form of government are not those seen in the entrusting of administration to the Throne in and following the Middle Ages [chūsei],[3] nor those of the British type of government in which "the sovereign reigns but does not rule"; nor yet are they the principles underlying joint government by a sovereign and his subjects; no more are they those underlying the policy of mutual independence of the legislature or the policy of binding everything under the law; but are entirely the basic principles of direct rule by the Emperor. This was not systematized as concerning laws relating to the form of government for a long while after its disruption following and including the Middle Ages, in spite of the fact that since the found-

[3]According to some Japanese historians the period from the reign of the Emperor Kōtoku till that of the Emperor Antoku (A.D. 645-1183). By reference to surviving authors of the Kokutai no Hongi it is known that this is the meaning of chūsei which was intended in this context.

ing of the Empire it has been the great law underlying the Imperial rule that runs throughout history in so far as regards the great august Will of the line of Emperors unbroken for ages eternal. But in the Meiji Restoration it was revived, and His Majesty set the matter forth clearly in the Constitution.

All the laws in the Imperial Constitution on form of government are but extensions and transmissions of this principle of direct Imperial rule. For instance, stipulations on the rights and duties of Sovereign and subject are different from those which exist among Western nations where a system of free rights serves to protect the inherent rights of the people from the ruler, for the stipulations are the fruit of the Emperor's fond care for his people and his great august spirit to provide them with equal opportunities for assisting the Throne without feelings of barrier. The triune subsistence, for example, of the Government, courts of justice, and the Diet, is different from the mutual independence of the legislature as it exists among Western nations, which aims at depriving the one holding sovereign power of judicial and legislative powers, giving recognition only to, yet at the same time curbing, his administrative power, with a view to restraining the powers of the ruler; for in our country segregation is not in respect of the rights of a ruler, but applies merely to the organs for the assistance of the direct Imperial rule, whose object is to make ever more secure the assistance extended to the direct rule by the Emperor. The deliberative assembly, too, is in a so-called democratic country, a representative organ of a people who are nominal rulers; while in a so-called monarchy, where the sovereign and the people govern the nation together, the assembly is a representative organ of the people whose object is to hold the caprices of the sovereign under restraint and to provide a means by which the ruler and the people may govern the nation together. Our Imperial Diet, on the other hand, is completely different; since it was instituted with the one object of providing the people with a means of assisting the Emperor's direct rule in special ways in regard to special matters.

OUR NATIONAL LAWS

Our national laws are one and all based on the Imperial House Law and the Imperial Constitution. Some of our statutes, laws, and regulations are established by direct Imperial sanction, while there are others that are established through the Emperor's authorization. There is, however, not one of all these statutes, laws, and regulations that does not find its source in His Majesty's august virtue. Granted that there are differences of various grades and orders in the spheres and degrees in the materialization of their substance, there is not one of these, after all is said and done, that is not a materialization of the Imperial House Law and the Constitution, which are oracles wherein the august injunctions of the Imperial Ancestor are transmitted. Hence, all our laws find their source in the Emperor's august virtue. As a consequence, our national laws are one and all expressions of our national entity.

Thus, our national laws are signposts to show the way by which the subjects may individually guard and maintain the prosperity of the Imperial Throne under His Majesty's august virtue, doing one's very best and so following His Majesty with awe. Hence, the basic reason for the subjects' respect for the Constitution and their observance of the national laws lies in their being true, loyal, and good subjects.

ECONOMY

Economy is the essence of a nation's material life; and commodities are necessary not only for the preservation of a people's natural life but are an indispensable factor in enhancing the Imperial prestige. Hence, it follows that the promotion of the nation's economic strength forms a vital basis for the development of our Empire.

Consequently, in the very beginning of the founding of the Empire, our Imperial Ancestor graciously introduced trades, and taught that economy, namely, industries, comprised one of the great national enterprises. The Emperor Jimmu was pleased to say,

If it brings profit to the subjects, how should it prove a hindrance to administrative activities?

while the Emperor Sujin [B.C. 97-30] said,

Agriculture plays the nation's basic role, and is the thing on which the people depend for their livelihood.

And we see that the successive Emperors constantly exercised concern for their subjects' occupations. However, our industries showed but little progress, because during the long feudal times occupations gradually became fixed and economy extremely rigid. Toward the close of the Edo Period many economists and leaders of economic living appeared on the scene. Among them in particular stands out the figure Ninomiya Sontoku [A.D. 1787-1856].[4] This Sontoku preached the doctrine of the merging of all things in one and of doing things in appreciation of divine and human favors, laid emphasis on the importance of hard work, behavior becoming to one's position in life, and of the spirit of sharing. This he expounded as the great Way concurring with the immutable law of the universe and as showing the fundamental Way of the Empire.

When our nation joined the nations of the world through the Meiji Restoration, it was strongly brought home to her that to develop her economic power by means of her agricultural products alone as in the past was a problem. Thus, since the Meiji Era many expressions in the way of counsels have proceeded from the Throne, with encouragement given for adopting modern Western technical methods of production. Also, exhortations were given to lay importance on thrift and diligence, while the way was paved for vocational education and encouragement was given to industrial activities. And in this manner His Majesty graciously exercised his concern for the promotion of the nation's wealth and for the felicity of his subjects. The subjects on their part complied well with His Majesty's great august Will, and through coöperation between official and subject and through fulfilling their mission by thrift and

---

[4] A popular moral philanthropist much quoted in Japanese text books.

diligence in the industrial fields, they have brought to fruition such national power as we see today. So rapid was the development that it has come to be looked upon by the world with utter amazement.

Our national economy is a great enterprise based on His Majesty's great august Will to have the Empire go on developing for ever and ever, and is a thing on which the subjects' felicity depends; so that it is not a disconnected series of activities aimed at fulfilling the material desires of individual persons, a doctrine expounded by Western economists. It is a thing in which the entire nation joins the Way of *musubi*,[5] each person fulfilling his duties according to the part he has been assigned to play. Agriculture, which developed early in our country, has meant the raising of crops through human efforts and the harmonious pursuit in the raising of crops between man and soil. This is the fundamental spirit of our national industries. Needless to say, commercial and industrial activities, though new to us, are things that must be engaged in with the same spirit.

It should be conceived that at the very basis of our modern economic activities there constantly runs this attitude toward industries that has come down to us since the founding of the Empire, in spite of the tremendous infiltration of Western ideas. This does not mean that every person in our country has always been awake to this spirit in his economic activities; nor does it mean that in all their industrial activities our people have been always free of harboring ideas of profit. But that the majority of those engaged in our national industries have harmoniously occupied themselves in their work in a spirit to do their respective duties faithfully and well rather than to be led merely by the idea of fulfilling their own personal material desires is a fact that can hardly be overlooked. It is for this very reason that a leap forward that vies with the world, as we have seen of late, has been made in our industrial society.

The attitude of mind which is based on the spirit of *musubi* and puts public interests before private ones, paying full attention to one's allotted duties and to being in harmony with others, has been

---

[5]See section dealing with this subject in Book I, Chap. IV.

an attitude toward industrial enterprises inherent in our nation; and it is a basic reason for the rise of a strong impetus in the world of industry, for encouraging initiative, stimulating coöperation, greatly heightening industrial efficiency, bringing about the prosperity of all industries, and for contributing toward the increase of national wealth. In our economic activities, we must in the future become fully awake to this particular attitude of mind toward industries, and with this consciousness strive more than ever to develop them. In this manner will economy conform with morals, and develop industries that are based on the Way and not on material profit, and be able to enhance the glory of our national entity in our economy.

MILITARY AFFAIRS

The manifestation of our national entity is just the same also in the case of our military affairs. Since ancient times the spirits of the deities in our country have fallen into two groups: the spirits of peace and the spirits of warriors. Where there is a harmonious working of the two, all things under the sun rest in peace, grow, and develop. Hence, the warrior spirits work inseparably and as one with the spirits of peace. It is in the subduing of those who refuse to conform to the august influence of the Emperor's virtues that the mission of our Imperial Military Forces lies; and thus we see the Way of the warriors that may be called Jimmu [Divine Warrior].[6] In an Imperial Rescript issued by the Emperor Meiji there is a passage which reads:

Our national entity which has paid tribute to chivalry since the days of Our Imperial Ancestors.

In the sixth year of Meiji [A.D. 1873], the Emperor promulgated the Conscription Law, bringing about universal conscription; and on January fourth in the fifteenth year of Meiji [A.D. 1882], His

---

[6]The first Emperor, so called, was a warrior; hence, what almost amounts to a play on his name.

Majesty issued an Imperial Mandate to the men of both the army and the navy, saying:

Our military forces shall be under the Emperor's command from generation to generation.

Again, His Majesty said by way of exhortation:

We are the Generalissimo of you men of the military forces. Wherefore, We shall depend upon you men as upon Our hands and feet and ye shall look up to Us as your leader. So shall the bonds of affection that bind us be made especially firm. Whether We shall be able or unable to respond to the grace of the heavenly deities and repay the goodness of Our Imperial Ancestors by guarding the nation shall depend on whether ye men of the military forces fulfill your duties or not. If at any time the prosperity of Our national glory should be endangered, ye shall indeed share the burden with Us. If our national chivalry is stirred to the surface and its glory is made known, We shall share the honor with you men. If ye shall all devote yourselves to your tasks and bend your powers to guard the nation, the people of our nation shall enjoy the blessings of peace for many years to come and make her national prestige greatly felt throughout the world.

This Imperial Mandate is read as if through it we could behold before us the Emperor's august virtue. Truly, the mission of the Imperial Forces lies in doing the Emperor's Will, in guarding the Empire[7] in perfect conformity with his great august wishes, and in thus exalting the national prestige. Our Imperial Forces have come to hold a position of responsibility in which their duty is to make our national prestige greatly felt within and without our country, to preserve the peace of the Orient in the face of the world powers, and to preserve and enhance the happiness of mankind, now that our Forces, in this spirit, have gone through the experiences of the Sino-Japanese and Russo-Japanese Wars and have joined the World War.[8]

---

[7]In the original manuscript. "Imperial Family" was substituted for "Empire" in later editions.

[8]The first World War (1914-1918).

Thus, we must observe His Majesty's commands to the effect that our people should "follow their allotted duties both in the literary and military spheres, the masses bending their whole strength to their individual tasks"; and so must we discharge our duties as subjects by guarding and maintaining the prosperity of the Imperial Throne which is coeval with heaven and earth, cooperating as one and rendering wholehearted service to the Throne.

CONCLUSION

Conclusion

We have inquired into the fundamental principles of our national entity and the ways in which it has been manifested in our national history. What kind of resolve and attitude should we subjects of the Japanese Empire now take toward the various problems of the day? It seems to us that our first duty is the task of creating a new Japanese culture by sublimating and assimilating foreign cultures which are at the source of the various problems in keeping with the fundamental principles of our national entity.

Every type of foreign ideology that has been imported into our country may have been quite natural in China, India, Europe, or America, in that it has sprung from their racial or historical characteristics; but in our country, which has a unique national entity, it is necessary as a preliminary step to put these types to rigid judgment and scrutiny so as to see if they are suitable to our national traits. That is to say, the creation of a new culture which has characteristics peculiar to our nation can be looked forward to only through this consciousness and the sublimation and assimilation of foreign cultures that accompanies it.

CHARACTERISTICS OF OCCIDENTAL IDEOLOGIES

Now, Occidental ideologies spring from Greek ideologies. Greek concepts, whose keynote is the intellectual spirit, are characterized by being rational, objective, and idealistic. Culture was shaped centering round cities, leaving to posterity philosophies and works of art rarely to be seen in human history; but toward the end of their days, individualistic tendencies gradually appeared in their ideologies and modes of life. Rome adapted and developed these Greek concepts in their laws, statecraft, and other practical fields, and at the same time adopted Christianity, which transcends the State. Modern concepts obtaining among European nations have arisen on the one hand with the aim of bringing about the Kingdom of Heaven on earth by reviving Greek ideologies and by claiming the liberation of individuals and the acquisition of their freedom in opposition to the religious oppressions and feudalistic despotism of the Middle Ages, while on the other hand their origin is seen in the attempt to put them into practice by carrying over the concepts that hold in high regard the qualities of universality and veracity that transcend the State as they existed in the Middle Ages. Hence, the astounding development of modern civilization that characterizes the history of the world, by bringing about the development of natural science—a civilization founded in the main on individualism, liberalism, and rationalism, in all the branches of education, scholastic pursuits, politics, and economics.

Human beings are real existences as well as historical existences linked with eternity. They are, furthermore, egos, as well as correlated existences. That is to say, their existences are ordained by a national spirit based on history. This is the basic character of human existence. Its real worth is found where this concrete existence as a people is kept in view and people exist as individuals in that very state. However, the individualistic explanation of human beings abstracts only one aspect of an individuality and overlooks the national and historical qualities. Hence, it loses sight of the totality and concreteness of human beings and deviates from the reality of human existence, the theories departing from actualities and running off into many mistaken channels. Herein lie the basic errors underlying the various concepts of individualism, liberalism, and their developments. The nations of the West have now awakened to these errors, and various ideologies and movements have sprung up in order to overcome them. Nevertheless, these ideologies and movements will eventually end in regarding collections of people as bodies or classes, or at the most in conceiving a conceptual State; so that such things will do no more than provide erroneous ideas to take the place of existing erroneous ideas, and will furnish no true way out or solution.

CHARACTERISTICS OF ORIENTAL IDEOLOGIES

Chinese ideologies introduced into our country were chiefly Confucianism and the philosophies of Lâo-tzŭ and Chuang-tzŭ.[1] Confucianism excels in its matter as a practical doctrine and is invaluable as a teaching. Consequently, it has filial piety for its basis of teaching, and this is owing to the fact that in China moral doctrines are founded with the family as the center. This filial piety has practicable qualities, but is not perfected as in our country as a national system of morals in which there is a merging of loyalty and filial piety. China bases her national morals on family morals, as witness the saying that loyal subjects come of families where filial piety is practiced; but because of revolutions which involve change of dynasties and transference of the throne, her loyalty and filial piety cannot become the morality of a historical, concrete, eternal State. Lâo-tzŭ and Chuang-tzŭ left this turbid world behind them and returned to nature, and harbored as their ideal an unsophisticated attitude of mind; which in the long run turned their doctrines into abstract notions that denied culture, so that they fell into individualism, not having stood on concrete and historical foundations. The followers of Lâo-tzŭ showed an inclination to live in seclusion away from the world like the Seven Wise Men of the Bamboo Grove,[2] and became disciples of a lofty hermit life. In a word, we may say that in that these thoughts are lacking in concrete, national foundations that develop historically, the philosophies of Confucius, Lâo-tzŭ, and Chuang-tzŭ, tend to become individualistic. But when adopted by our country, these philosophies shed themselves of their individualistic and revolutionary elements; so that Confucianism in particular was sublimated and assimilated into our national entity, bringing about the establishment of a Japa-

---

[1]Combined in what is usually considered Taoism, although, in a narrow sense, Taoism concerns only the teachings of Lâo-tzŭ.

[2]This same idea of a retreat from the world in the cultural or philosophic sense in the West is conveyed by the English expression, "ivory tower."

nese Confucianism, and contributing greatly toward the development of our national morality.

Buddhism in India has ascetic and intuitive aspects; but as it is a product of imaginative and unrealistic racial traits, it is meditative, unhistorical, and transcends the State. However, in its assimilation by our nation, it was sublimated and fused into our national spirit, contributing much toward enriching the fountainhead of the State.

CREATION OF NEW JAPANESE CULTURE

To put it in a nutshell, while the strong points of Occidental learning and concepts lie in their analytical and intellectual qualities, the characteristics of Oriental learning and concepts lie in their intuitive and ascetic qualities. These are natural tendencies that arise through racial and historical differences; and when we compare them with our national spirit, concepts, or mode of living, we cannot help recognizing further great and fundamental differences. Our nation has in the past imported, assimilated, and sublimated Chinese and Indian ideologies, and has therewith supported the Imperial Way, making possible the establishment of an original culture based on her national entity. Following the Meiji Restoration Occidental cultures poured in with a rush, and contributed immensely toward our national prosperity; but their individualistic qualities brought about various difficulties in all the phases of the lives of our people, causing their thoughts to fluctuate. However, now is the time for us to sublimate and assimilate these Occidental ideologies in keeping with our national entity, to set up a vast new Japanese culture, and, by taking advantage of these things, to bring about a great national development.

In introducing, sublimating, and assimilating Occidental cultures, it is necessary at the outset to inquire into the essence of Occidental institutions and ideologies. If this were not done, elucidation of the nature of our national entity might fall into abstractions that have lost sight of realities. Notable characteristics that mark modern

Western cultures are the spectacular developments of the natural sciences which are based on positivism and of the material civilization which is their fruit. Further, in the fields of mental sciences, too, there is the same precision and logical systematization and the shaping of unique cultures. Our nation must increasingly adopt these various sciences, and look forward to the advancement of our culture and national development. However, these scholastic systems, methods, and techniques are substantiated by views of life and of the world peculiar to the West, which views are due to the racial, historical, and topographical characteristics of the Occident. Hence, in introducing these things into our country, we must pay thorough attention to these points, scrutinize their essential qualities, and with the clearest insight adapt their merits and cast aside their demerits.

VARIOUS REFORMS

An examination of our national trends since the Meiji Restoration shows that there are those who, casting aside the traditional spirit, have immersed themselves in Western ideas; and those who, while holding to their historical faith, have fallen a prey to dualistic concepts by accepting the scholastic theories of the West at their face value and without giving them sufficient scrutiny. And what is more, there are those who have done this without being conscious of the fact. Again, the result has been a considerable intellectual gap between the intelligentsia who have markedly come under the influence of Occidental ideologies and the common people. Thus, such a situation has given rise to various knotty problems. The fact that such things as communist movements, which at one time were popular, or the recent question of the organ theory in regard to the Emperor, have from time to time been taken up by a group of scholars and some of the intelligentsia, is an eloquent proof of the situation then prevailing. Although communism of late appears to have fallen into decay and the organ theory to have been exploded, these things have by no means been thoroughly solved. So long as further progress is not made in the investigation of the true nature of Western ideologies in all fields, and their sublimation and assimilation by means of our national entity remains unrealized, it may be difficult to reap genuine results.

Everyone seems to realize that extreme Occidental ideologies and studies in general, such as communism and anarchism, fall wide of our national entity; but little attention is paid as to whether those ideologies and studies that are not extreme, such as democracy and liberalism, really accord with our national entity or not. Now, when we consider how modern Occidental ideologies have given birth to democracy, socialism, communism, anarchism, etc., we note, as already stated, the existence of historical backgrounds that form the bases of all these concepts, and, besides, the existence of individualistic views of life that lie at their very roots. The basic characteristics of modern Occidental cultures lie in the fact that an individual is looked upon as an existence of an absolutely independent being, all cultures comprising the perfection of this individual being who in turn is the creator and determiner of all values. Hence, value is laid on the subjective thoughts of an individual; the conception of a State, the planning of all systems, and the constructing of theories being solely based on ideas conceived in the individual's mind. The greater part of Occidental theories of State and political concepts so evolved do not view the State as being a nuclear existence that gives birth to individual beings, which it transcends, but as an expedient for the benefit, protection, and enhancement of the welfare of individual persons; so that these theories have become expressions of the principles of subsistence which have at their center free, equal, and independent individuals. As a result, there have arisen types of mistaken liberalism and democracy that have solely sought untrammeled freedom and forgotten moral freedom, which is service. Hence, wherever this individualism and its accompanying abstract concepts have developed, concrete and historical national life became lost in the shadow of abstract theories; all States and peoples were looked upon alike as nations in general and as individuals in general; such things as an international community comprising the entire world and universal theories common to the entire world were given importance rather than concrete nations and their characteristic qualities; so that in the end there even arose the mistaken idea that international law constituted a higher norm than national laws, that it stood higher in value, and that national laws were, if anything, subordinate to it.

The beginnings of modern Western free economy are seen in the expectation to bring about national prosperity as a result of free, individual, lucrative activities. In the case of the introduction into our country of modern industrial organizations that had developed in the West, so long as the spirit to bring about national profit and the people's welfare governed the people's minds, the lively and free individual activities went very far toward contributing to the nation's wealth; but later, with the dissemination of individualistic and liberal ideas, there gradually arose a tendency openly to justify egoism in economic managements and operations. This tendency gave rise to the problem of a chasm between rich and poor, and finally became the cause of the rise of ideas of class warfare; while later the introduction of communism brought about the erroneous idea which looked upon economy as being the basis of politics, morality, and all other cultures, and which considered that by means of class warfare alone could an ideal society be realized. The fact that egoism and class warfare are opposed to our national entity needs no explanation. Only where the people one and all put heart and soul into their respective occupations, and there is coherence or order in everyone's activity, with their minds set on guarding and maintaining the prosperity of the Imperial Throne, is it possible to see a healthy development in the people's economic life.

The same thing holds true in the case of education. Since the Meiji Restoration our nation has adapted the good elements of the advanced education seen among European and American nations, and has exerted efforts to set up an educational system and materials for teaching. The nation has also assimilated on a wide scale the scholarship of the West, not only in the fields of natural science, but of the mental sciences, and has thus striven to see progress made in our scholastic pursuits and to make education more popular. The progressive spirit that sought knowledge all over the world, in obedience to the Charter Oath in Five Articles, and by breaking away from old abuses, brought about rapid progress in this sphere, too, thus reaping tremendous results. However, at the same time, through the infiltration of individualistic concepts, both scholastic pursuits and education became liable to be taken up with a world in which the intellect alone mattered, and which was isolated from historical and actual life; so that both intellectual and moral culture drifted into tendencies in which the goal was the freedom of man who had become an abstract being and the perfecting of the individual man. At the same time, these scholastic pursuits and education fell into separate parts, so that they gradually lost their synthetic coherence and concreteness. In order to correct these tendencies, the only course open to us is to clarify the true nature of our national entity, which is at the very source of our education, and to strive to clear up individualistic and abstract ideas.

Thus, modern Occidental ideologies that have infiltrated all fields of education, scholastic pursuits, politics, and economics, amount to nothing short of individualism. Hence, it must be acknowledged that individualistic cultures have achieved the awakening of individuals to a sense of their individual values and stimulated the elevation of individual faculties. Nevertheless, as actualities in the West show, individualism virtually provokes the setting up of an individual against an individual and classes against classes, and foments many problems and disturbances in the national and social life. In the Occident, too, many movements are now being carried out to revise individualism. Socialism and communism, which are types of class individualism, and which are the opposites of so-called bourgeois individualism, belong to these movements, while recent ideological movements, such as that known as Fascism, which are types of nationalism and racial consciousness, belong to this category.

In order, however, to correct the faults brought about by individualism in our country and to see a way out of the deadlock which it has created, it would be utterly impossible to do this, if we adopted such ideas as Occidental socialism and their abstract totalitarianism wholesale, or copied their concepts and plans, or else mechanically excluded Occidental cultures.

OUR MISSION

Our present mission as a people is to build up a new Japanese culture by adopting and sublimating Western cultures with our national entity as the basis, and to contribute spontaneously to the advancement of world culture. Our nation early saw the introduction of Chinese and Indian cultures, and even succeeded in evolving original creations and developments. This was made possible, indeed, by the profound and boundless nature of our national entity; so that the mission of the people to whom it is bequeathed is truly great in its historical significance. The call for a clarification of our national entity is at this time very much in the fore; but this must unfailingly be done by making the sublimation of Occidental ideologies and cultures its occasion, since, without this, the clarification of our national entity is apt to fall into abstractions isolated from actualities. That is to say, the adoption and sublimation of Occidental ideologies and the clarification of our national entity are so related as to be inseparable.

The attitude of the Japanese in the past toward the cultures of the world has been independent and yet at the same time comprehensive. Our contributions to the world lie only in giving full play more than ever to our Way which is of the Japanese people. The people must more than ever create and develop a new Japan by virtue of their immutable national entity which is the basis of the State and by virtue of the Way of the Empire which stands firm throughout the ages at Home and abroad, and thereby more than ever guard and maintain the prosperity of the Imperial Throne which is coeval with heaven and earth. This, indeed, is our mission.

APPENDICES

I

ABRIDGED GENEALOGY OF THE GODS

Based on the genealogy in K. Asakawa (ed.), *Japan: From the Japanese General History,* vol. VII of the *History of Nations Series* (Philadelphia: Morris, 1906). Honorifics have been eliminated for simplicity.

Spontaneously created Gods

Izanagi (male)   Izanamı (female)

Amaterasu   Tsuki-yomi   Susano-o

Amano-Oshihomimi   Amano-Hohi   Ohkuninushı

Ninigi   Kotoshironushi

Hikohohodemi   Hosuseri

Ugayafukiaezu

Itsuse   Inagi   Mikenu   Emperor Jimmu

                                                          Existing Imperial
                                                          Line

II

WORDS FOR EMPEROR, COUNTRY, AND PEOPLE USED IN THE KOKUTAI NO HONGI

EMPEROR

Akitsukami (Marvelous Deity; lit., Lucid Deity.)

Akitsumikami (Deity Incarnate; lit., Manifest-August-Deity.)

Amatsukami no Miko (August Child of the Deities in Heaven.)

Arahitogami (Deity Incarnate; lit., Manifest-Man-Deity. Used principally in regard to a living Emperor.)

Aramikami (Another reading for the Chinese compound which is also read *Akitsumikami*. See above.)

Dai Gensui (Generalissimo.)

Hijiri (Sacred One.)

Kimi (The Chinese character, which is *kun* in Japanized Chinese pronunciation, is read *Kimi* when standing alone and appears frequently in classical literature. Ruler; Sovereign.)

Kimi (The Chinese character, which is ō in Japanized Chinese pronunciation, is read *Kimi* when standing alone and appears frequently in classical literature. Monarch.)

Kinjō Tennō Heika (H.M. the Present Emperor.)

Kunshu (Ruler; Sovereign; Sovereign Lord.)

Ohkimi (The Chinese compound *daiō* or *taiō*, e.g. Alexander *Daiō*, is given the Japanese reading *Ohkimi* and appears frequently in classical literature. Lit. Great King.)

COUNTRY

Amatsukami no Kuni (Lit., Country of Heaven-spirits.)

Ame no Shita (The Chinese compound *hakkō* is an old name for Japan when given the Japanese reading *Ame no Shita*. Lit., Eight Corners.)

Ametsuchi (The Chinese compound *rikugō*, "*Rik-ugō*, is an old name for Japan when read as *Ametsuchi* as well as *Rikugō*. Lit., Six Quarters; i.e., the then known world or Japan.)

Chūgoku (Lit., Central Land. The name is also applied to China.)

Dai Nihon Teikoku ("Great" Japanese Empire.)

Hasshū (Eight Islands.)

Hinomoto no Kuni (Land of the Rising Sun.)

Kokka (State; nation.)

Kōkoku ("Japanese" Empire; lit., Imperial Country.)

Kokudo (Homeland.)

Kuni (Country.)

Kuni no Uchi (Another Japanese reading of the Chinese compound *rikugō*, and the same as *Ametsuchi*, q.v.)

Mikuni (Country; honorific literary form.)

Mizuho no Kuni (Land of Fresh Rice-ears.)

Nihon (Nippon.)

Nihon no Kuni (Land of Japan.)

Ohdo (Imperial Land.)

PEOPLE

Bammin (The people; i.e., the whole nation. Lit., ten thousand subjects.)

Chōmin (The people; i.e., the whole nation. Lit., a trillion subjects.)

Hasshū Minsei (The people of the Eight Islands.)

Jimmin (The people; subjects.)

Jinshin (Subjects.)

Kokumin (Nation; the people.)

Kunitami (Japanese reading, i.e., *kun-yomi*, for *kokumin*, q.v.)

Minjin (Same as *Jimmin*, the characters being reversed without affecting the meaning.)

Minzoku (Race; hence *Yamato minzoku*.)

Mitami (The people honorific literary form.)

Nihon-jin (A Japanese; The Japanese.)

Nippon-jin (Same as *Nihon-jin*.)

Ohmitakara (In *hiragana*, i.e., cursive phonograms. Subjects. It is of doubtful etymology, some saying it refers especially to farmers and others saying it means the Emperor's subjects.)

Ohmitakara (Chinese compound, lit., one hundred surnames, is given the Japanese reading *Ohmitakara*.)

Ohmitakara (Chinese compound, lit., source source, is given the Japanese reading *Ohmitakara*.)

EMPEROR

Ohkimi (The Chinese compound *taikō* is given the Japanese reading *Ohkimi* and appears frequently in classical literature. Lit., Great Emperor.)

Ohkimi (The Chinese compound *taikun* is given the Japanese reading *Ohkimi* and appears frequently in classical literature. Lit. Great Sovereign. When applied to a *shōgun* of the *Tokugawa* Period diplomatically, it is pronounced *taikun*.)

Shujō (Lit., High Lord.)

Sumera (The Chinese compound *tennō* is given the old Japanese reading *Sumera* and appears frequently in classical literature.)

Sumeragi (in *hiragana*, i.e., cursive phonograms. Emperor.)

Sumerogi (in *hiragana*, i.e., cursive phonograms. Emperor.)

Tennō ("Heavenly" Emperor.)

Tennō Heika (H. M. the Emperor.)

Tenshi (Child of Heaven.)

Chin ("We" as used by the Emperor.)

Sumera Ware ("We" as used by the Emperor. Lit., We the Emperor.)

COUNTRY

Oh-yashima (Great Eight Islands.)

Oh-yashima no Kuni (Land of Great Eight Islands.)

Shikishima no (Poetical pillow words in characters. Lit., Of the Scattered Islands.)

Shikishima no (Poetical pillow words in *hiragana*, i.e. cursive phonograms. Lit., Of the Scattered Islands.)

Shinkoku (Divine Land, Land of the Gods. Used particularly by Shintoists and ultra-nationalists.)

Shinshū (Divine Islands; Land of the Gods. Used particularly by Shintoists and ultra-nationalists.)

Tenka (Under Heaven; the realm.)

Toyoashihara no Mizuho no Kuni (Abundant Reedplain Rice-ear Land.)

Toyoashihara no Nakatsu Kuni (Abundant Reedplain Central Land.)

Urayasu no Kuni (Land of Peace.)

Yamato (In *hiragana*.)

Yamato (In characters. Lit., Great Harmony.)

Yasukuni (Peaceful Land.)

PEOPLE

Okuchō (The people; the multitude. Lit., one hundred million one trillion.)

Okuchō Shimmin (Lit., one hundred million one trillion subjects. See *Okuchō* and *Shimmin*.)

Sekishi (Subjects, in the sense of the Emperor's subjects. Lit., babes; sucklings; children.)

Shimmin (Subjects. Lit., subjects subjects, or subjects people.)

Shin (Subjects.)

Sōsei (The people. Lit., "multitudinous" people.)

Tami (The people; subjects.)

Tamibito (The people; subjects. "Japanese" hoi polloi.)

III

STATISTICS ON RELIGIOUS GROUPS

(Based on best available Japanese official statistics for 1937, date of
publication of the *Kokutai no Hongi*)

Christianity	Churches	Members
Roman Catholic	265	96,000
Presbyterian	304	37,500
Methodist	246	33,600
Episcopal	242	31,400
Congregational	165	27,000
Others (Baptists, Friends, Seventh Day Adventists, etc.)	844*	90,000*
Total	2,066	315,000

*Includes Russian Orthodox Church: 91 Churches, 12,927 members
in 1938 (1939 *Yearbook of Religion*.)

Buddhism	Temples	Adherents
Hossō	41	19,000
Ji	494	350,000
Jōdo	7,124	3,646,000
Kegon	27	23,000
Nichiren	4,998	7,376,000
Ritsu	23	58,000
Shingon	11,947	9,117,000
Jōdo Shinshū	19,815	13,327,000
Tendai	4,438	2,141,000
Yūzū Nembutsu	357	153,000
Sōtō	14,244	6,848,000
Zen Rinzai	5,984	2,530,000
Ohbaku	500	120,000
Total	69,992	45,708,000

Sect Shinto	Adherents
Fusō	648,000
Konkō	1,120,000
Misogi	343,000
Shinshū	775,000
Shintō Honkyoku	1,272,000
Taisei	728,000
Tenri	4,385,000
Jikkō	436,000
Kurozumi	566,000
Mitake	2,048,000
Shinri	1,489,000
Shūsei Ha	430,000
Taisha	3,373,000
Total	17,613,000

State Shinto

By law all Japanese (estimated at 70,000,000) were required to profess acceptance of the official national cult.

Confucianism

No statistics available but most Japanese accepted in some degree as a moral philosophy.

IV

[official translation]

Know ye, Our Subjects:

Our Imperial Ancestors have founded Our Empire on a basis broad and everlasting and have deeply and firmly implanted virtue; Our subjects ever united in loyalty and filial piety have from generation to generation illustrated the beauty thereof. This is the glory of the fundamental character of Our Empire, and herein also lies the source of Our education. Ye, Our subjects, be filial to your parents, affectionate to your brothers and sisters; as husbands and wives be harmonious, as friends true; bear yourselves in modesty and moderation; extend your benevolence to all; pursue learning and cultivate arts, and thereby develop intellectual faculties and perfect moral powers; furthermore, advance public good and promote common interests; always respect the Constitution and observe the laws; should emergency arise, offer yourselves courageously to the State; and thus guard and maintain the prosperity of Our Imperial Throne coeval with heaven and earth. So shall ye not only be Our good and faithful subjects, but render illustrious the best traditions of your forefathers.

The Way here set forth is indeed the teaching bequeathed by Our Imperial Ancestors, to be observed alike by Their Descendants and the subjects, infallible for all ages and true in all places. It is Our wish to lay it to heart in all reverence, in common with you, Our subjects, that We may all thus attain to the same virtue.

The 30th day of the 10th month of
the 23rd year of Meiji [October 30, 1890]

[Imperial Sign Manual]   [Imperial Seal]

OFFICIAL MINISTRY OF EDUCATION POLICY ON INSTRUCTION

[Based on Ministry of Education Laws (*Mombuhōrei*) and enunciated by Ministry of Education Order No. 2, March 25, 1943. Translated from an official copy of Order No. 2.]

I. ETHICS

Policy for Instruction.

1. In obedience to the spirit of the Imperial Rescript on Education, the fundamental principles of our national entity shall be clarified and the students shall be thoroughly taught the true import of faithfulness and loyalty and of guarding and maintaining the prosperity of the Imperial Throne.

2. A spirit of reverence for the deities and one's ancestors and of public service shall be cultivated by guiding the students in walking the Way of the Empire in all phases of national life.

3. The characteristics peculiar to the Empire's administration, military affairs, economy, and culture, which find their source in our national entity, shall be taught; and a spirit to strive for the prosperity of the nation and for the creation and development of her culture shall be fostered.

4. The students shall be taught so that they may contribute to the clarification of the fundamental principles of the Way of the Empire by inquiring into those features that characterise Western and Oriental ideologies and cultures.

5. The students shall be made conscious of the Empire's mission in the Far East and the world and of the vital nature of national defence; and a spirit and intellect worthy of a great nation shall be cultivated.

Remarks:

Particular attention shall be exercised in regard to the Imperial Rescript on Education, the Oracle, and to sacred precepts, making their meaning clear and causing the students to observe their purport.

II. JAPANESE

Policy for Instruction.

1. The reasons why Japanese is an expression of national thought and sentiment and is at the same time its plasmic product shall be explained; and an ability to understand it and to express oneself correctly shall be cultivated and a respect for the language fostered.

2. Through a study of Japanese classical literature, the students shall be taught to understand the traditions of the Empire and its literary expressions, and development of modes of life as a people and creation of the Empire's culture shall be fostered.

3. Through a study of classical Chinese, the students shall be taught to understand the ideologies and cultures of the Empire and of East Asia and the ways in which they are expressed, so that they may contribute to the cultivation of our national spirit.

III. HISTORY

Policy for Instruction.

1. Through a clarification of the Empire's nuclear position, the students shall be made to grasp the histories of the Empire and of the East and the West as a related whole, and a basis for their activities as nationals shall be fostered by widening their historical outlook and by increasing their knowledge.

2. The reasons why historical accomplishments are manifestations of the spirit of the founding of the Empire shall be explained in detail; light shall be thrown on the prevailing state of affairs and their significance in regard to every historical period on the basis of the continuous nature of the Empire's progress, and its developments in relation to world history studied; thus causing the students to appreciate the great life of the Empire and thus deepen their national consciousness.

3. The reasons for the differences between the history of our Empire and those of other nations shall be explained fully and the fundamental principles of our national entity fully clarified; and in view of conditions within the nation and abroad, appropriate guidance shall be given in regard to historical facts about national defence and industries by laying emphasis on our people's expansion abroad.

4. By presenting a comprehensive view of the rise and fall and prosperity and decline of the nations and races of East Asia and the world up to the present time and by delving especially into the activities of and historical facts about the peoples of East Asia and the truths about European and American invasion of East Asia, the historical significance of the establishment of Greater East Asia shall be elucidated and the mission of our Empire taught.

5. Through an investigation of the traditions of Japanese culture, the prosperity and decline as well as the characteristics of the cultures of the East and the West shall be explained, and a spirit to create a new culture with our Empire as the nucleus shall be fostered.

IV.   GEOGRAPHY

   Policy for Instruction.

1. The geography of Japan and of foreign countries shall be taught as a related whole with our Empire forming the nucleus, and the foundation of the people's activities shall be nurtured by cultivating a geographical outlook necessary to the subjects of our Empire.

2. The students shall be led to inquire into the conditions of our Land and the people's mode of living, as well as into their mutual relationship, on the basis of an outlook of the Land peculiar to the Empire, and thus shall a spirit to protect the Land be fostered.

3. The students shall be made conscious of the Empire's mission through a study of the geographical features peculiar to foreign lands of East Asia and of the world and through deepening their knowledge in regard to our Land and its state.

4. The students shall be led to inquire into natural features and modes of living at home and abroad, while the characteristics of our Land and its state shall be explained, and they shall be made conscious of the geographical significance of the establishment of Greater East Asia and the founding of a system for thorough national defence.

VI

IMPERIAL RESCRIPT DENYING DIVINITY OF THE EMPEROR

[Official English translation reproduced in the United States **Department** of State Publication No. 2671, "Occupation of Japan: Policy and Progress." The Imperial Rescript was issued on New Year's Day, 1946.]

In greeting the new year we recall to mind that the Emperor Meiji proclaimed as the basis of our national policy the five clauses of the charter at the beginning of the Meiji era. The charter oath signified:

(1) Deliberative assemblies shall be established and all measures of government decided in accordance with public opinion.

(2) All classes high and low shall unite in vigorously carrying on the affairs of State.

(3) All common people, no less than the civil and military officials, shall be allowed to fulfill their just desires so that there may not be any discontent among them.

(4) All the absurd usages of old shall be broken through and equity and justice to be found in the workings of nature shall serve as the basis of action.

(5) Wisdom and knowledge shall be sought throughout the world for the purpose of promoting the welfare of the Empire.

The proclamation is evident in its significance and high in its ideals. We wish to make this oath anew and restore the country to stand on its own feet again. We have to reaffirm the principles embodied in the charter and proceed unflinchingly toward elimination of misguided practices of the past; and, keeping in close touch with the desires of the people, we will construct a new Japan through thoroughly being pacific, the officials and the people alike obtaining rich culture and advancing the standard of living of the people.

The devastation of the war inflicted upon our cities the miseries of the destitute, the stagnation of trade, shortage of food and the great and growing number of the unemployed are indeed heartrending; but if the nation is firmly united in its resolve to face the present ordeal and to see civilization consistently in peace, a bright future will undoubtedly be ours, not only for our country but for the whole of humanity.

Love of the family and love of country are especially strong in this country. With more of this devotion should we now work toward love of mankind.

We feel deeply concerned to note that consequent upon the protracted war ending in our defeat our people are liable to grow restless and to fall into the slough of despond. Radical tendencies in excess are gradually spreading and the sense of morality tends to lose its hold on the people with the result that there are signs of confusion of thought.

We stand by the people and we wish always to share with them in their moment of joys and sorrows. The ties between us and our people have always stood upon mutual trust and affection. They do not depend upon mere legends and myths. They are not predicated on the false conception that the Emperor is divine and that the Japanese people are superior to other races and fated to rule the world.

Our Government should make every effort to alleviate their trials and tribulations. At the same time, we trust that the people will rise to the occasion and will strive courageously for the solution of their outstanding difficulties and for the development of industry and culture. Acting upon a consciousness of solidarity and of mutual aid and broad tolerance in their civic life, they will prove themselves worthy of their best tradition. By their supreme endeavors in that direction they will be able to render their substantial contribution to the welfare and advancement of mankind.

The resolution for the year should be made at the beginning of the year. We expect our people to join us in all exertions looking to accomplishment of this great undertaking with an indomitable spirit.

VII

OFFICIAL POSITION THAT THE *Kokutai* HAS NOT CHANGED

[The following passage appeared in the booklet, *Exposition on the New Constitution,* published by the Japanese Imperial Cabinet, November 1946.]

In regard to the change that has taken place in the Emperor's position, the Diet and other groups have seen lively discussions asking whether through the New Constitution our national entity has not been altered. The question of national entity is one lying at the basis of a written Constitution, and is not a matter directly related to its clauses, being a matter that should properly be left to individual judgment and scholastic theories; so that our purpose here is to introduce the Government's explanation briefly and to leave the matter to individual judgment.

The term *national entity* can mean many things, but it is appropriate to interpret its correct meaning as *basic characteristics of the nation.* So interpreted, national entity forms the foundation of the nation's existence, and its destiny is common with that of the State; so that if this national entity were to suffer change or loss, the State would at once lose its existence. We should have to conclude that even if a new State were to be established, there would no longer be anything common in the nature of the old State and the new. When we look upon national entity in this way and in its relation to our country, we can say that in a word it means the immutable and solemn fact that the Japanese people look up to the Emperor as if he were the centre of their adoration, on the basis of the link that deep down in their hearts binds them to him, that the entire nation is united thereby, and that this forms the basis of Japan's existence.

When we look back soberly on how, on the other hand, many scholars in theories of public law have affirmed that the unilineal[1] Emperor's over-all control in matters of sovereignty constitutes our national entity, and on how they have declared Articles I to IV of the Meiji Constitution to be a so-called stipulation of our national entity, we cannot help feeling

---

[1]*Bansei ikkei no,* literally, "of a line unbroken for ages eternal."

that there has been, as it were, a certain bondage to institutional characteristics that have varied with the times since the days of Meiji; so that
rightly these things should be understood as matters belonging rather to
forms of government than to national entity. Consequently, national entity, that is, the form of our government, has of course undergone a
great change through the late revision.

That the recent revision of the Constitution was carried out in accordance with the provisions of Article LXXIII of the Meiji Constitution
can be understood without any feelings of inconsistency only when the
immutability of the national entity, the consequent oneness of the State,
and further the continuity of the Constitution are laid down as premises.
Moreover, there is, in relation to the problem of national entity, the question of the place of sovereignty in our country, as regards which we
present the views of the Minister of State Without Portfolio, Mr.
Kanamori.

The principle that sovereignty rests with the people raises the
problem whether there has been a change or not in the position of
sovereignty. If we inferred on the basis of a scholastic theory held
hitherto which claims that sovereignty rests with the Throne, the
natural conclusion reached would be that sovereignty has been trans-
ferred to the people. Nevertheless, according to another view, sovereignty has always rested with the entire nation, the Emperor having been the controlling organ of national rights. This principle
which holds that sovereignty rests with the people is a thing to
which the people were hitherto not fully awake, having appeared in
the form of a theory which claimed that sovereignty rested with the
State, etc. The fact is that we have now entered into a period of
awakening to this point. Even in the past the Emperor's position
was accompanied with an understanding on the part of the people,
so that if we looked upon the matter coolly on this basis, we could
say that the intrinsic qualities of the sovereignty resting with the
people have existed in the past. In short, the question is whether the
change is actual or apperceptive; but whichever it may be there is a
change. But as for myself [Minister of State Without Portfolio, Mr.
Kanamori] I think the latter concept is the right one.

The foregoing is the Government's view concerning our national entity and sovereignty, but heated discussions have been witnessed in both Houses of the Diet. Particularly in the House of Peers law scholars banded themselves together to ask the Government if the national entity had not undergone any change, but the Government stood by their belief that what had suffered a change was the form of government and not the national entity. These differences of views will probably remain in the future as a scholastic problem regarding the interpretation of the New Constitution.